No Limits –

Unlimited

No Limits – Unlimited

Photocopiable materials for teachers of English as a foreign language

By Dan Lamb

With short stories contributed by Jaimina Bodalia, Cheryl Campbell, Daniel Goodwin, Jane Grimshaw, and Carolyn Kiff

fygleaves

www.nolimits-unlimited.com

ISBN 978-0-9550780-4-0
First edition

PUBLISHED 2007 BY FYG Perspectives
AN IMPRINT OF FYGLEAVES LTD
FYG STUDIO, WEST EALING, UK W13 9JR
www.fygperspectives.co.uk   www.fygleaves.co.uk
COVER: WILLIAM RUSSELL © FYGLEAVES LTD

Cover with thanks to: Zhe Wu, Tesfariam Woldu, Juliet Kulanyi, Basir Ahmad, Alexander Weiser, Ramona Krupa, Anna Mazurcak, and Leila Ali.

Printed and bound by CPI Antony Rowe, Eastbourne

With thanks

especially to Kate:
without all your support this book would not have been possible.

To all those who have encouraged me in this project

and to Paula Clossick, Marian Dawson, and Marc Jordan
for your constructive input
and
in appreciation of
your understanding of the fun and dedication that is required in good teaching.

Contents

Section G: Grammar

Section R: Reading

Section S: Speaking and Discussion

Section W: Writing

Section T: Tests and Reviews

Index

Introduction to the activities in this book

The aim of this book is to provide teachers with practical resources which can be used in class, if necessary at short notice, and to create opportunities for students to review topics of EFL and ESOL study, through materials which can be utilised in any number of various ways.

It is not intended as a curriculum of activities, but as a useful bank of supplementary and review worksheets. The more materials a teacher has available, the better: students need a lot of feeding... with immeasurable portions of continual consolidation.

How to use this book

The book has been designed to combine the benefits of a lightweight pocket book with ease of photocopying: all the worksheets enlarge directly to A4 size, and once you have made a single copy it is easy to make extra adaptations or use that as a master to photocopy a class set.

Materials have been grouped by language skills, in generally ascending level of difficulty, with a teacher's notes page to accompany each related set of worksheets.

Prominent boxes at the top of teacher's notes pages show when a worksheet has a particular link to another resource within a different section, while specific grammatical topics can be located immediately via the index.

As well as giving tips for less experienced teachers, the notes pages offer guidelines for all the teaching materials included, and list answers for activities where appropriate, whilst maximising the ratio of worksheets to notes.

Throughout the book, ideas are included for adaptations of the resources for students of different levels, and teachers are encouraged to add to the worksheets as they see fit: allow this book to inspire you to experiment, and to grow in teaching creativity, as you tailor these materials to the needs and context of your own students.

No Limits

The beauty of designing resources is that other teachers may use them in a completely different way to the one who designed them – and so there are no limits to the ways these worksheets can be used.

Experienced teachers using this book will be able to find their own ways of using these materials, and I realise some will use these resources as a last-minute stopgap when they are thrown into a class they have not had time to prepare for; if so I am glad to have helped in this way!

Unlimited

New teachers will also be able to gain a full understanding of the intentions behind the materials, enabling them not only to use those worksheets which are applicable to their setting, but also to be inspired to make their own resources.

This book suggests aims, techniques, and formats which can be adapted to the language and vocabulary being taught in any classes of any size, any age and any level.

The strength of these worksheets is not in colourful pictures and complicated design: any one of these pages could be re-created on a word processor, but they are a collection of proven teaching techniques and methods which I share with others just as others have shared their ideas with me.

I trust that people will be able to pick and choose from these materials as they please, and where there are shortcomings, they will be able to reproduce unlimited and newly-improved versions of the materials for their own classes.

This book will have served its lasting purpose if it sparks off ideas, which are the unlimited aspect of English teaching. Teaching should never be boring!

Dan Lamb, 2007

Teaching and Learning: we never stop!

Learning theory

There are lots of books which discuss the best theories of language learning and even propose new ways of teaching English, and this is a subject that can be studied in tremendous detail. As far as this book is concerned, however, the main things to remember are that you need to:

- Engage the class and make the lesson fun
- Focus on the main lesson aims and try not to be too diverted
- Continually monitor the progress of all students
- Consolidate and build with ongoing lesson-to-lesson review

It is assumed that teachers using this book will already be aware of the main TEFL principles such as maximised use of pair and group work, low TTT (Teacher Talking Time), 'task before text' (explaining an activity before handing out the worksheets), and demonstrating an example to get students started (making sure students have understood their instructions by using an OHP or whiteboard to model an activity first). These principles are not therefore recounted for every worksheet.

It is important also to remember that although a teacher teaches a group, it is individuals who learn: for this reason issues such as learning styles, differentiation, and Individual Learning Plans are discussed in the book, as these are an important means of keeping the teacher's focus on the needs of each individual rather than those members of the class who tend to shout out an answer to your questions. Furthermore, it must not be forgotten that one of the key aspects of teaching is the motivational ability of encouraging students in their own self-study.

The two aspects of language skills

Language is ultimately about intertwining the use of vocabulary and the use of grammar, and no matter how far a student may advance in one of these aspects, their overall progress will be limited by how far they advance in the other. Students need to be encouraged that both must go hand in hand.

The difference between reception skills and production skills

Meanwhile it is necessary to distinguish between listening and reading (reception skills) which tend to consolidate with use, and speaking and writing, which require the student to reproduce what they have learned. Hence when teaching any combination of vocabulary and grammar, it is not enough to get a student to the stage where they can understand it being used in a listening or a reading context: a full check on their learning will involve assessing whether the student can use the target vocabulary and grammar in their speaking, and whether they can use it in their writing.

Skills within skills

In addition, there are different skills within the area of, for example, reading: gist reading, scanning and full comprehension. It is important to be aware of these distinctions, and set work according to the level of the students. The same skills apply in listening, for gist, for specific information, or for the full meaning, and it is important not to discourage students through unrealistic expectations, especially when using authentic texts.

With regard to production skills, it is also important to recognise that if a student is able to convey meaning, despite making mistakes along the way, they have achieved the primary purpose of communication. Perfection is not always a realistic level to aim for! Mistakes which actually give a different meaning to the one intended by a student are critical, however, and these always need to be highlighted in error correction and review activities.

Meeting individual needs

Within every class some of the students will work better in certain skills than others, and the theoretical job of the teacher is to ensure that their stronger students are never held up, and simultaneously that their weaker students are not left behind.

One way of addressing this objective, known as differentiation, is to give different students adapted versions of the worksheet you are using. It is also helpful to give feedback to students in smaller groups, or individually if possible, but if this is to happen in class you must ensure that other students are being kept busy: as one means of enabling this theory to work in reality, most of the worksheets supplied here include extension tasks and activities.

Nothing works without classroom management

Of course, differentiation, including extension activities, requires good classroom management – but if you don't have good classroom management from the start you will struggle to teach anything for the rest of the course.

The validity of pair work

Students may not like working in pairs at first, but this is another form of meeting individual needs since students are helping each other by working in this way. (Therefore, if a strong student is working with a weaker student, it is important for them to realise that they themselves will consolidate their own learning by, for example, explaining language points.)

Students should also understand that the purpose of paired speaking activities is to give them an opportunity to self-focus on accuracy and in this situation it should not matter if a stronger student is working with a weaker student. (Spoken work, which does not lead to any additional marking, also makes an excellent extension activity, and when it tends to pair up higher-level students who have finished a task earlier than others, they can then also work together in listening out for each other's spoken mistakes.)

The importance of consolidation and review

It is not enough to learn something one week and then forget it by disuse: the process of learning involves continual consolidation and so teaching also becomes an ongoing cycle of providing opportunities for review. This will include picking up on issues that 'come up' as it is students' authentic mistakes which provide the most personalised context for learning. However, it is important to let students develop confidence without interrupting them or highlighting their mistakes all the time.

Why are we doing this?!

No, I don't mean why are we as teachers putting ourselves through the stresses of teaching! What I mean is, do you always understand why you are doing a certain activity in class, and do your students also understand why when applicable? This is one of the reasons why many teachers suggest that it is helpful to make the lesson aims clear to students at the beginning of a class, and it is often helpful to ask a class why they are doing a certain activity, to help them focus on its benefits.

Individual progress by individuals

Ultimately, it is the learner who must learn: a teacher can only encourage their students, explain and demonstrate, and direct them towards the work they need to do. It is therefore a key component of our teaching that we train our students in study skills and emphasise the lasting importance of their own learning.

If they will not do their part, there is a limit to what the teacher can actually do to help: for this reason you must not feel responsible for any of your students' failings, as long as you have done all you can to motivate and equip them.

The EMMA cycle

One tool that I have found helpful in reflecting whether I am meeting the needs of each individual student is my 'EMMA' checklist:

equip – motivate – monitor – address

Am I equipping each student appropriately?
Am I motivating students to learn?
Am I monitoring each student's progress?
Am I addressing individual needs as a result?
Am I then equipping them accordingly...? etc

It is by responding to your students, with all the skills that make you a person as opposed to a robot, which will make you a successful teacher. We ourselves never stop learning how to teach.

Section N | New Students

'Getting to know you' activities

When you first take on a new class, the most important thing is to set the tone and thus get the right balance between being strict enough to make sure students will listen to you when you are explaining something, and laid-back enough to let them know they will have fun in class and enjoy their learning.

The activities in this section are designed for three main objectives which you should bear in mind in all of the initial sessions you have with a class: for you to get to know your students a little, for the students themselves to get to know each other, and for you to get an initial idea of the level of your students and the differences of level within your group.

You may work in an organisation which uses a diagnostic test, designed to show the teacher the areas each student may need to focus on, but even if you don't carry out an official test, you will do this subconsciously to some extent and you will need to decide how you are going to manage this process on an ongoing basis. This will depend on a number of issues, especially the number of students in your class and their own learning aims. It is important to make sure that your students leave the room feeling they have used the time well: the wider the level of students within your group, the harder this is, but you must motivate students by ensuring that the class is not too easy for anyone, nor too difficult.

About You, N1

This worksheet reviews basic written sentences, with the spoken work possibly functioning as an extension activity: it is always important to be aware who is likely to finish a worksheet sooner than the rest of the class and to make sure that you can then give them meaningful work to do: extension activities are therefore one valid means of achieving differentiation, which is an attempt to juggle the needs of different students working at different levels, or at a different pace, all at the same time.

N1 About You

Put the words in order to make sentences. Then write down whether the sentence is true or false in your life, and ask your partner.

True Or False?
You   Your partner

1. before studied have English I

2. married near live and am we in flat I a here

3. a busy have job I because difficult time free it study my is to in

4. speak I very think I English can well

5. email moment have I an address at don't the

6. write use going homework computer English to am a my I to

7. to studying me help reason get I am a job the English good is

When you have finished discuss your answers with your partner and find out some more information about him or her.

Pair Work with Many Partners, N2-N4

As discussed in the introduction to this section, the N worksheets are intended especially to provide a way for students to get to know each other and for you as the teacher to establish the levels you are working with.

Students will generally sit with those they feel most comfortable with, but it is important that you also move them around in the early stages of a course so that they are able to interact with other class members right from the beginning.

For this reason, it is worth introducing a variety of activities which allow the students to mill around the room using adapted questionnaires such as the deservedly ubiquitous 'Find someone who...' concept.

N2, N3 and N4 are intended to prompt a slightly more detailed level of conversation between partners who have not sat together before. The advantage of a worksheet like these is that it gives students initial ideas about what to ask each other, and even if the level of a worksheet may seem a little easy for your group, it should help students to pick up momentum for their own personalised conversation.

Once students have then got a variety of ideas fresh in their minds, there is no reason why they should not be able to carry out 'free' conversations if you then mix up all the partners again.

Meanwhile, as you monitor the pairs by listening to sections of their conversations, you will hear some spoken errors which you can note down and feed back to the whole group when appropriate: either in a short grammar review before mixing the groups up again, or as the focus of a follow-up lesson when you have had a chance to prepare materials.

Another technique I enjoy using with a new class is to invite the students to ask me questions: I tell them they can ask anything they like, with the proviso that I will only answer it if they ask the question with correct grammar and pronunciation...

N2 | Questions in Many Tenses

Can you fill in the gaps correctly in the right tense? When you have finished, ask your partner some more questions.

1 *Your personal details*

What_____your name?
Where_____you from?

2 *Your Daily Life*

What time_____you wake up?
What_____you do before you go to work?

3 *At the moment*

Hi,_____ you free right now?
What_____ she eating?

4 *General Questions*

What time_____the bank open?
Where_____Jill and Jo live?

5 *In the past*

How_____you get to work yesterday?
And_____you late?

6 *At a specific time in the past*

Who_____you talking to at 8pm last night?
What_____he doing when you called him?

7 *About an experience*

So, _____you ever slept in a tent?
And_____you ever stayed up all night?

8 *Plans for the future*

So,_____you working next week?
What_____you going to do this weekend?

N3 Corrections

Which sentences are correct? In each group of three sentences there is one mistake: can you find it?

1. She doesn't have a car.
   She doesn't got her book.
   She hasn't got any children.

2. Do you like studying English?
   Do you like fish and chips?
   Do you like play football?

3. London is biggest city in England.
   Dublin is the capital of Ireland.
   Paris is a city in France.

4. What time our next lesson starts?
   What time does the canteen close?
   What time does the shop open?

5. My house is small.
   My wife car is red.
   My sister's a nurse.

6. When do you get up?
   What is your job?
   What job do your brother do?

7. Liz and Tom don't eat fish.
   Polly no speak French.
   I don't like sports.

8. Do you have got a pen?
   Do you have any children?
   Have you got your book?

When you have finished, re-write each sentence in its box to correct the mistake. Then write down some more questions to ask your partner.

N4 | Various Sentences

1 *First, complete these sentences with information about yourself using verbs with either 'to' or 'ing'.*

I'm scared of _to fly / flying_____ .
a | I need _____ .
b | I'd like _____ .
c | I enjoy _____ .
d | I hate _____ .
e | I've decided_____ .

2 *Use the correct form of the adjective to complete the sentences below.*

a | The USA is _____ than England. (big)
b | Wales is the _____ country in Britain. (small)
c | Cars are _____ than bicycles. (fast)
d | English is _____ than Maths. (interesting)
e | London is the _____ part of England. (expensive)

3 *Underline the correct form of verb in the following sentences.*

a | I <went / have been> to America last year.

b | I <used to play / have played> tennis every day when I was a child.

c | I <lived / have lived> in London for six months now.

d | I <watched / was watching> TV last night when the phone rang.

e | She <returned / has returned> to Australia last week.

4 *On the back of this page write five sentences about what you have done during the last year, and what you enjoyed most.*

5 *Then write five sentences about your hopes and plans for the future.*

6 *Finally, discuss your sentences in sections 1, 4, and 5 with a partner.*

Timelines Questions, N5

Fortunately, students tend to be interested in their English teacher, especially if you and they are from different countries. This leads to good opportunities in class for reviewing questions, and discussion between students finding out about each other.

You will need to add some events in your life to the worksheet before you photocopy the class set, such as:

I got married
I became a teacher
I bought a car
I was born
I went to university

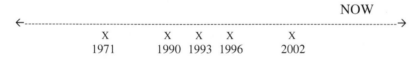

You can start the activity by putting the students in pairs and asking them to guess which year your events took place.
Draw the timeline on your white board and when you elicit the students' guesses, fill in the events clearly, writing them up in the third person, as below.

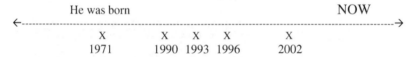

At this stage you can ask students to make a list of five events in their lives, without showing the dates to their partner. Only when they have understood the concept of guessing the year that events took place in their partner's life are you ready to hand out the worksheet: very often the success of an activity depends on meticulously going through the instructions step by step, and at this stage you may want to model the activity again by rubbing out the answers on your board and asking the students to repeat the first matching activity on the worksheet.

Ensure that students understand the 'About me' section should look like your original example, and then they are ready to start guessing the year of each of their partner's events.

Match the events in your teacher's life with the correct year

NOW

←--→

Now write down five events from your life and your partner will try to guess the correct year.

<u>About me</u>

NOW

←--→

In this section you can guess the year of the events in your partner's life.

<u>About my friend</u>

NOW

←--→

Finally, discuss some of the other events in your life with your partner.

Teacher's Aims and Record of Work, AA

Good teaching is not just about the classroom: it is a planning, measuring, and tracking process of challenging and encouraging your students. If done properly, this will require a level of organisational ability and you should expect to be paid for your planning and administration time in order to fulfil this role.

Before you start teaching you should have a curriculum or a Scheme of Work which gives details of all the subject matter your school or organisation expects you to cover with your class, and you should therefore be able to form an overview of your intended teaching for each week, month, or term, in advance.

Within this overview, you will then need to plan each individual lesson so that you are clear in your own mind what objectives you want your students to have achieved, as a step on their way to their final goal. What's more, it is one of the most significant parts of your job to assess how well each student achieved those aims, and therefore to decide how much review is necessary either as an immediate follow-up or at a later stage.

Individual teachers will keep this information according to their own preferences but the Record of Work template opposite is intended to prompt you to keep the necessary basic records that will enable you to carry out this function.

Note that if you teach a number of classes at the same level it is particularly important to keep a record of the work covered with each group: it is surprisingly easy to get confused about which worksheets you have used with which class, and to end up trying to give one class the same materials twice! Meanwhile it is vital to keep a note if any particular student was absent when you covered a key element of your curriculum, or if anyone was struggling with the learning objective, so that you can review this material with that student as appropriate later.

| AA | Aims and Record of Work | CLASS: SHEET NUMBER: |

Date	Class Aims & Objectives	No. Of Students and absentees	Work Done, Materials Used, & Notes					

Making the Paperwork Your Friend not Your Enemy, A1-A3

The suggestions in this section form what I would consider to be key strands for a teacher's administration file, in the planning, measuring and tracking process.

The danger of too many 'good ideas' in this area is an avalanche of administrative tasks – the downside of public sector teaching in the UK nowadays – but I would encourage you to pick and choose the ways that work for you.

A1 is a learning styles questionnaire to help the teacher see how individual students function best. Different students will prefer the use of various kinds of learning materials and activities, and it is important to incorporate visual prompts and hands-on work in your classes, while this worksheet is also intended as a platform for you to emphasise to each class member that other students may function best in a different learning style to their own.

If your students are internet users, this questionnaire can also be accessed on the website www.nolimits-unlimited.com where each student can enter their answers and the score will be calculated automatically.

For teachers of students without internet access, you can calculate a score according to this marking scheme.

		VISUAL	AUDITORY	KINAESTHETIC	READ-WRITE
I use my hands a lot when I speak	K			K	
I often read things aloud to myself to help me understand the meaning	A		A		
I find it helpful to see information written down for me to copy it	V	V			V
I like making things rather than writing things	K			K	3 MINUS K VALUE
It distracts me if there is music or talk in the background when I am trying to work or study	A		A		
When I learn new spellings I need to look at the words and write them down more than once	V	V			V
I like being able to move around when I am talking on the telephone	K			K	
I can remember spoken information quite well even if it is not written down	A		A		3 MINUS A VALUE
I find diagrams and pictures the most helpful way of remembering information	V	V			
I find a mind map more useful than making a list if I am planning an essay	V	V			
I am good at describing the sounds of a place I have visited	A		A		
I find it hard to sit still for a long time	K			K	

A2 and A3 are templates of a student feedback form, and a self-assessment form for students to return when they submit an assignment: hand it out when you set the task, with the left-hand column filled in to highlight specific criteria, and the results will enable you to compare the student's perception of their progress with your own. Then use this in discussion with the student about how they can address any areas identified for improvement.

A1 | Learning Styles

Every student may have different preferences in the way they remember things best, and it is helpful for your teacher to know what helps you.

Learning Style Questions Please enter 3 if you agree strongly, 2 if you agree, 1 if you disagree, and 0 if you disagree strongly.	Your answer here: enter 3 if you agree strongly, 2 if you agree, 1 if you disagree, and 0 if you disagree strongly.
I use my hands a lot when I speak.	
I often read things aloud to myself to help me understand the meaning.	
I find it helpful to see information written down for me to copy it.	
I like making things rather than writing things.	
It distracts me if there is music or talk in the background when I am trying to work or study.	
When I learn new spellings I need to look at the words and write them down more than once.	
I like being able to move around when I am talking on the telephone.	
I can remember spoken information quite well even if it is not written down.	
I find diagrams and pictures the most helpful way of remembering information.	
I find a mind map more useful than making a list if I am planning a piece of writing.	
I am good at describing the sounds of a place I have visited.	
I find it hard to sit still for a long time.	

When you have finished, discuss with a partner whether you like to learn new words by seeing them visually, listening to them repeatedly, or speaking them out. Does it also help you to write them down?

Ask the other students in your class about their answers to the questions above. How many different preferences are there?

A2	Student Feedback Form

It is very helpful for me as your teacher to know if there has been anything in my classes which you think was very helpful, or not useful.

Please answer the questions below, and return the form anonymously.

What do you think about your lessons generally?

Can you give an example of anything that you found:

Very useful for you

Not very useful

Of the work we have done recently, which do you think was:

the easiest?

the most difficult?

Is there any way that you think your classes could be improved?

Do you have any other comments?

| A3 | Self-assessment Form |

Assessment name:	
Date given:	
Date submitted:	

In my work I have...	My self – assessment (e.g. good, or it could be better)
...used correct punctuation.	

Student's Comments
(e.g. is there anything you think you need to practise more?)

Date:

An Individual Learning Plan, A4

Any teacher will aspire to help each student with their personal learning needs, and the aim of an Individual Learning Plan is to create a two-way discussion formalising this process.

The teacher needs to arrange a time to meet individually with each student for a discussion of progress 'so far' and to set targets for the student to work towards. In real life, a lack of time is a significant limiting factor, but it is worth implementing this practice with students at regular intervals during a course.

Good teaching is a combination of both motivating students in self-study and paying professional attention to their individual needs, and the ILP is a key opportunity to emphasise these twin aspects of a student's learning.

Any number of targets can be agreed between the teacher and the student, which may relate primarily to academic learning, or to personal matters which are hindering the individual's ability to study. However, it is important to specify what the student's targets are and when they are due to be completed, and these are therefore the main aspects of the ILP template provided.

It may be that some students would respond better to a cluster of smaller, more manageable targets, while other learners would prefer to be given a project which encompasses a variety of different skills. However, it is important not to be too vague with targets such as: 'the student will practise speaking in English with his friends outside class more often': unless a mechanism such as a student diary is agreed, achievement of a target like this, and any benefits gained from it, can be impossible to verify.

The most important thing is that students are not made to feel over-burdened by their ILP targets, but that they understand how this work will benefit their progress.

If used properly, the ILP can contribute significantly to the process of motivating students. It is not possible to prioritise any individual student in normal class time but if you have grasped the principle of the ILP you will be able to show each learner that their individual needs are being addressed in this way.

A4 Student's Individual Learning Plan

Name_____.

Every student needs to practise their English by working outside class as well as during lessons.

My target:

Date set:

Date to be checked: Checked:

My next target:

Date set:

Date to be checked: Checked:

My next target:

Date set:

Date to be checked: Checked:

My next target:

Date set:

Date to be checked: Checked:

Student Progress Form, A5

This is another means of tracking students' progress, which may be used in conjunction with setting ILP targets, or as a regular review.

As with the self-assessment form, A3, this may be updated with different details as and when appropriate.

An example of possible criteria within each of the learning areas is shown here. You may also want to use this format at the end of each teaching unit or topic to provide a summary of what you have covered.

Learning Area	Comments
Study Skills and Grammar Time Management Homework completion	
Speaking and Listening Pronunciation Words per minute Sentence stress	
Spelling and Vocabulary Verb tense spellings Parts of the body	
Reading and Writing Using reference information Punctuation in written work	

Prioritise People not Paperwork

Remember that your administrative tasks are to help you track and review student progress. You spend that time marking so you can highlight areas for improvement, and you need to keep a record of students' marks and their work so that you can measure, and show them, their improvement during the course.

However, it is possible to spend too much time on the paperwork and not enough time on the ultimate purpose behind it – feeding back to your students to equip them for their ongoing progress. If we don't use our marking and the paperwork as a means to help our students, we are wasting much of our time... so use your admin time to help you focus on students' needs, and don't let this section snow you under with paper for the sake of it.

| A5 | Student Progress Form |

Name _____   Date _____ .

Learning Area	Comments
Study Skills and Grammar	
Speaking and Listening	
Spelling and Vocabulary	
Reading and Writing	

Student's Comments:

Rhyming Words, P1-P4

Correct pronunciation of basic English sounds is vital if a speaker is to be understood, and the use of rhyming words is especially helpful for students in pronouncing vowel sounds. Although speakers of different native languages may have additional difficulties with certain English consonants, they can make great progress if pronunciation of their vowels is clear.

P1: some suggested words for dictation. Choose or add in words most relevant to the level of your students.

Rain train rail snail pain paint wait
Boat coat road loaf toast soap groan float
Light night midnight tonight sight might right bright
Feet see meet tree free green keep sleep sweet three sheep
           greed sheet bleed
Eat meat peas beans cream tea sea seat mean beach dream
Food moon room soon spoon zoo (cook look foot good)

This and the following worksheets should lead you into further discussion of rhyming words, highlighting the fact that there can be different ways of spelling the same sound, and enabling you to work on other activities such as poems and limericks if appropriate.

P2a and P2b link pronunciation with spelling practice. The choice of two worksheets enables you either to select the most appropriate worksheet for your class, or to cover the same material in a differentiated manner within the same group. Note, however, that you may also want to fill in an answers sheet to photocopy instead of carrying out board-centred feedback...!

P3, by contrast, is designed to show that words ending in the same spelling pattern do *not* necessarily rhyme – with apologies to all English students! e.g. 'now' and 'low', never mind 'bow'...

P4 in this section deals with some difficult consonant clusters such as 'three' – and try out 'twelfth' with your students...!

P1	Rhyming Words

Can you match the rhyming words in these two columns?

hope	rain
scene	soap
plane	night
June	green
bite	moon

Notice that in each case the rhyming words use a different spelling pattern.

Listen to the words your teacher will read out and try to list them in the correct group.

'-oo' like moon   '-ee' like green   '-ea' like eat

'-ai' like rain   '-ight' like night   '-oa' like soap

Which Spelling?

Can you match the rhyming words in these two columns?

first	saw
for	crowd
hurt	skirt
tall	burst
loud	crawl

Even though we may know how to pronounce a word, that doesn't always mean we will spell it correctly. Can you choose the correct spelling for the words in each of the columns below?

'-ur' or '-ir'	*'-ou', or '-ow'*	*'-or', '-aw', or '-al'*	
ch___ch	l__d	b__l	f__k
b__d	r__nd	h__l	
f__st	h__se	sm__l	f__l
h__t	d__n	st__m	
Sat__day	f__nd	w__l	y__n
g__l	m__se	t__n	
sh___t	br__n	sp__t	c__n
Th__sday	cl__d	h__se	
d__t	p__nd	c__l	b__n
t__ key	t__n	d__n	
sk__t	s__nd	l__n	c__k
b___n	cr__n	sh___t	
b__st	gr__nd	p__k	f ___d

If you have finished, try and use as many of these words in a conversation with your partner as possible.

P2b | Which Spelling?

Can you match the rhyming words in these two columns?

first	saw
for	crowd
hurt	skirt
tall	burst
loud	crawl

Even though we may know how to pronounce a word, that doesn't always mean we will spell it correctly. Each of the words below has two letters missing: can you choose the correct spelling?

The missing letters are '-ur', '-ir', '-or', '-ou', '-ow', '-aw', or '-al'

ch___ch	w__l	f__nd
b__d	y___n	m___se
sp__t	d__t	c__k
b__l	l__n	br___n
f__st	sk__t	cr__l
Sat__day	c__l	t___key
g__l	b___st	f__l
f__k	p__k	cr___n
Th__sday	h__t	h__l
c___n	l__d	sm___l
st__m	r__nd	cl__d

If your vocabulary is very wide, you might have found that some of the words above could have two answers. All of the words below also have two possible answers: can you work them out?

b___n	h__se	sh__t	t__n	d__n
b___n	h__se	sh__t	t__n	d__n

Can you use any of these words in a conversation with your partner?

P3 | Pronunciation of '-ea' and '-ow'

Can you match the rhyming words in these two columns?

cheap	bed
now	toe
head	sweep
know	meat
sweet	cow

Notice that the same vowel spelling might still be pronounced differently, and that different spelling patterns can be pronounced the same.

List the words in the box below in the correct columns.

'-ow' like now   *'-ow' like know*   *'-ea' like cheap*   *'-ea' like head*

---

down   meat   beans   blow   sea   low
    heavy   eat   town   beach   bread   how
snow   slow   mean   crowd   ready   cream
    brown   seat   dream   now   yellow   peas
instead   tea   spread   grow   window   dread

Shhh! I'm thinking.

Some words begin with two (or sometimes three) consonants before the first vowel in the word. How many patterns can you think of?

<u>*'Ch', 'Sh' and 'Th'.*</u>

These combinations are special because they can come at the start or end of a word. Can you add 'ch', 'sh' or 'th' as the correct beginning or ending to these words and list them in the columns below? Then practise pronouncing these words with your partner.

> *Words with only one answer:*
> mu__,   fi__,   __en,   __ut,   __arp,   pin__,
>   mun__,   __eese,   __ree,   Mar__,   ru__,
> twelf__,   __oulder   mo__,   __ing,   __ime,   __irsty

> *Words with two answers:*
> wi__, wi__, __op, __op, __ip, __ip, __ink, __ink, __ank, __ank

<u>'ch'</u>   <u>'sh'</u>   <u>'th'</u>

chin   punch   shin   dish   thin   cloth

Vowel Sound Pronunciation, P5-P7

Although these worksheets build the material up in a step-by-step manner, I find that some students seem to 'get' this concept quicker than others and you may need to reassure those who find it hard going at first.

Having understood the concept of rhyming words, students are now asked to concentrate on the vowel sound alone, and this is a more difficult test of their pronunciation ability. This work may therefore lead to some valuable coaching of vowel pronunciation so that words such as ran and run, for example, can be clearly distinguished in students' listening and speaking.

It is also interesting for students to see that there is a pattern in these pronunciation rules which they may not have come across before.

Meanwhile it is worth pointing out that people with different accents will pronounce their vowels slightly differently.

P5, as far as possible, uses introductory words that are meant to be words the students will have come across previously, which should help them focus on pronunciation issues, and note that this worksheet links back specifically to P1.

P6 extends the vocabulary used to demonstrate the principle involved, and note that it also incorporates further word combinations such as win-wine, plan-plane, and tub-tube.

P7 develops the theme by including additional variations for pronunciation of 'a' and 'o' (with apologies to any of my friends with northern accents!) and includes a further box of words which is intended to show students that now they can even pronounce words they may never have seen before.

Depending on how well your students respond to these activities, there are various opportunities to lead on into further pronunciation work such as breaking longer words down into syllables.

P5 | Adding an 'e' in Pronunciation

Look at the five words below and read them aloud:

mad   pet   bit   hop   cut

Now think what happens if you add an 'e' to the end of the words:

made   Pete   bite   hope   cute

What pattern can you see here?
Can you think of any other words which follow the same rules?

Look at the following words and read them aloud.

dog, five, name, pig, tune, cat, bed, bone, sun, scene

Now can you write these words in the correct columns below?

'a' like mad   'e' like pet   'i' like bit   'o' like hop   'u' like cut

'a' like made   'e' like Pete   'i' like bite   'o' like hope   'u' like cute

If you can think of any other words like this, try and add them to the correct column.

| Matching Pronunciation of Vowels

Now look at these words and add them to the correct column below:

box   cake   dog
    bus   six   hate
hat   hot   home
    like   sad   win
ten   tube   cup
    wine   plan   top
mat   plane   tub
    smoke   ran   red
white   hit   gene

<u>'a' like cat / mad</u>   <u>'e' like pet / bed</u>   <u>'i' like bit / pig</u>

<u>'o' like hop / dog</u>   <u>'u' like cut / sun</u>

<u>'a' like made / name</u>   <u>'e' like Pete / scene</u>   <u>'i' like bite / five</u>

<u>'o' like hope / bone</u>   <u>'u' like cute / tune</u>

Can you match the vowel sounds of the words in these two columns?

cat	brother
dog	hat
son	last
father	shop

Some of the words in the box below may be new for you. List them according to their pronunciation in the columns below:

> mother hen leg plate mud cot bag milk shop made bled grass bike
> game led ice soft done sat wind slept on man time big ham broke him
> bath prize yet sit help nest shape went rope shine Monday gate fun
> London jump other lip rather bite glass clap run nine fox up must
> home dune case joke nose nod front save fat none snake dome fate
> muse mumps shed dene path slide mule nasty dote cede cube shun

'a' like cat / mad	'a' like made / name	'a' like father / last

'e' like pet / bed	'e' like Pete / scene	'i' like bit / pig

'i' like bite / five	'o' like hop / dog	'o' like hope / bone

'o' like son / brother	'u' like cut / sun	'u' like cute / tune

The gapfills at the top of the page are effectively difficult riddles, so feel free to give the students clues if necessary, or play them as hangman or an equivalent game on the white board:

When the stars are <u>out</u>, they are visible, but when the lights are <u>out</u>, they are invisible.
A fat <u>chance</u> is no more likely than a slim <u>chance</u>.

Since the second half of this worksheet is also quite difficult, students could be led into the activity by first working with the words in the box to make sentences of their own: in feedback you would thus be able to prepare them by highlighting the possible different meanings of each word.

Meanwhile, if you have class members who need a challenge – (!) make it even more difficult as below. Students have to put the words in order as well as match the correct word from the box.

the to such not beautiful lady a could.	close
on they to boat how about had a the.	object
door for too it something the was to to.	row
bandage doctors around the quickly a his.	produce
the takes our all pride in farm we.	polish
if table we to are the it going use must we first.	wound
the up the the strong road hill began to in.	present
I eyes in when saw my in the there my were painting.	tears
present these all need while people we to the are.	wind

P8 | Seeing Double

Can you complete this sentence twice by using the same word twice?

When the stars are _____, they are visible, but when the lights are _____, they are invisible.

Now can you add a different word to complete this sentence?

A fat _____ is no more likely than a slim _____.

Now consider this. Sometimes a word can be pronounced differently, with a different meaning, even though it has the same spelling: For example, which word could be added twice to this sentence?

She must be able to because she a letter to me last night.

read	produce	object	present	row	
polish	wound	tears	close	wind

Now choose a word from the box which can be added twice to each of the incomplete sentences below. Can you complete all the sentences?

The lady could not to such a beautiful.

They had a on the boat about how to.

Something was too to the door for it to.

The doctors quickly a bandage around his.

Our farm takes pride in all the we.

If we are going to use the table we must it first.

The road began to up the hill into the strong.

There were in my eyes when I saw the in my painting.

We need to the while all these people are present.

Vocabulary Review, V1-V3

V1-V2 Link to P5-P6

I originally designed the first of these worksheets for low level students but I include them here as I have found many 'minimal preparation' uses for them which work with other students too!

Lines are left for lower-level students to copy the text as handwriting practice, although just for fun the worksheet could alternatively be used by students writing blindfolded or with their wrong hand – e.g. a right-handed student using their left hand.

V1 asks students to recognise that each word is made up of only one syllable, and then challenges them to try the same thing.

V2 specifies the task of adding words to the sentences, and depending on the level of your class you may insist that these words are of two, three, or more syllables. The extension task here sets students the difficult task of writing sentences entirely made up of words with at least two syllables. (Try it yourself first! – you may decide to allow, for example, one exception per sentence.)

These worksheets would also lead nicely into a round-the-class speaking game where students each say one word in turn to add meaning to a sentence, with the catch that each word must be of only one syllable. Once you have demonstrated the rules this can be played in groups, and you could also allocate certain group members with the task of always using a two (or three!) syllable word when it is their turn.

V3 addresses the issue of spelling numbers correctly and includes a review of ordinal numbers, as well as maths vocabulary and the construction of thousands, and millions.

It would be easy to cover the use of a decimal point if appropriate for your class, and this can lead to useful number dictations, where students have to write down the numeric version of a high number with an outrageously long string of decimals. A similar effect can be achieved by dictating 'international' phone numbers.

V1 | Not as Easy as it Looks!

Look at the sentences below. What is special about every word?

The cat likes milk.

_____

Ten men sat on a box.

_____

The pig wore a big hat in the wind.

_____

"Stop! It's too hot!" said the sad man.

_____

I ran to the top of the hill then I went to bed and slept.

_____

The dog bit my lip and I hit him with a bag.

_____

Can you write any more sentences like this?

_____

_____

_____

V2 | Only One Syllable?

Here are some more sentences with words of only one syllable. Can you think of any other words you could add to make the sentences longer?

The sun is up.

_____

The bus must stop for him.

_____

He kicked the cup in the mud.

_____

The cat licked the box and got stuck.

_____

I ran to the back of the nest and was sick.

_____

The dog had a stick and my sock.

_____

Can you write any sentences which do not use any words of one syllable?

_____

_____

_____

Numbers, Dates and Maths!

Look at the numbers below. First, match them together.

twenty-five	96	fifty-one	16
thirty-four	42	sixty-eight	79
eighty-three	25	sixteen	60
ninety-six	83	sixty	68
forty-two	34	seventy-nine	51

Now write the correct spellings for the numbers below.

14	23
62	57
36	41

Can you spell and pronounce these ordinal numbers used for dates?

7th	11th
18th	3rd
22nd	5th
31st	12th

Do you know these maths symbols? Can you match them correctly?

plus	X
minus	=
multiplied by (times)	−
divided by	+
equals	÷ (or /)

Now try to write out the calculations below, following the example.

16 plus seventeen $16+17 = 33$ thirty-three
245 plus thirty-eight
485 minus nineteen
44 multiplied by eight
756 divided by seven
98745 minus nine thousand
2456731 plus ninety-nine

Spellings and Alphabetical Order, V4-V6

Some students struggle more with spellings than others, and addressing their difficulty, including finding techniques to help them learn, is therefore a key issue for teachers. An English dictionary is a valuable tool for students to check their spellings, but bear in mind that if someone doesn't know a spelling already, they will not necessarily be able to find it in the dictionary!

Unfortunately for students, they will have already noticed that there are countless anomalies to the apparent rules of English spelling, and that in the end the only way to learn them is to buckle down in self-study. What is important from the teacher's point of view is to help students recognise spelling patterns in words where they do exist, and to help them find a method of learning which works for them.

V4 is a review of the rules of alphabetical order, since this is a vital skill when a student is using a dictionary or an index; note that the extension activity for faster students allows you to spend time with others who may need a recap, and as always, you can make a worksheet more difficult if required: e.g. for advanced students, insist that the sentences they write use the specified words in alphabetical order *within* each sentence...

V5 is a simple technique you can use with any words that you want to cover in a spellings review: provide the students with a list of mistakes which they have to correct.

V6 is a development of this theme, whereby students have to recognise which words are correct and which are mistakes.

If you give students a spelling test of your own, you may want to follow it up using their authentic mistakes with the V5 or V6 format – or both, possibly as a differentiated review activity.

Note also that dyslexia is a diagnosable condition and that you might observe tell-tale signs in a student's work, such as consistently mixing letters up in the wrong order, which may alert you to the possibility that the student is dyslexic; if so they should be eligible for a certain level of leeway, as well as specialist support if it is available.

V4 | Alphabetical Order

Look at the words next to each box and list them in alphabetical order.

For example: apple   ⟶   1. and
and   2. apple
ate   3. ate

baby	1 baby
children	2
black	3
car	4
but	5
cat	6

Can you make a sentence that includes as many of these words as possible?

_____
_____
_____
_____

new	1
sister	2
mobile	3
sitting	4
have	5
homework	6
floor	7
must	8

	1
older	2
two	3
their	4
got	5
home	6
orange	7
ginger	8
of	9
house	10
hot	

V5 Correct the Mistakes

Can you correct the spelling mistakes in these common words?

usefull

everythink

brekfast

gratefull

usauly

adresse

hugge

wendsday

docter

chenge

clothse

yestrday

riting

childrn

shopingg

hopeles

expencive

beuatiful

computr

dificult

becusse

saterday

always

expeirence

maggazin

langages

Circle the words below which contain spelling mistakes: can you write the correct spellings for these words?

excelent	brigde
famous	building
grammar	candel
recepsion	sugar
leissure	littel
finnaly	traditions
dangerous	unpopullar
complan	variety
faitfuly	disarster
sinserelly	adrress
forward	mariage
probleem	computer
especially	hungrey
clouthes	therstiy
probablly	dictsionary
importent	neccesary
blod	flouuers

Look-Cover-Write-Check, V7

Although by no means the only way to learn spellings, this is an important method which students should be encouraged to try in their self-study.

This LCWC worksheet is designed to be folded, and needs to be used in conjunction with a blank page for covering the list of words when the student is testing themselves. Clearly, the idea is that once a student has grasped the concept, they would be able to repeat the procedure at home for any appropriate words using their own list and paper.

Having looked at the top word, the student then covers it up and tries to replicate the spelling in the space provided. Then they are able to check the spelling and re-write it correctly if appropriate, before continuing to the next word in the list.

Once the student has completed the list of spellings, or maybe a smaller chunk of them, they can then fold the worksheet lengthways, approximately along the second dotted line, so that the typed list of words is still visible, but their first spelling attempts and corrections are hidden under the flap created by folding the page: they can then repeat the look-cover-write-check procedure on the reverse of the paper folded into place.

The aim of the worksheet is therefore to introduce students to the concept of a learning technique, which they can then adapt to suit their own preference: instead of L-C-W-C, some students might prefer to write the spelling once or more times, for example, before covering it up (W-C-W-C) – or they might develop their own alternative method, according to their own learning style. Students need to recognise the limitations of their own memory, however, and the need for ongoing self-review: there is no point spending a long time learning a list of spellings one day, only to have forgotten them the next week.

Ultimately the aim is that students can develop their own self-study preference and then use it to improve their spellings. It may surprise you how many students have never used any particular technique for learning spellings and so it is important to model a method such as this in class.

V7 | Look, Cover, Write and Check: Spellings

Word list	*First, test your spelling in this space*	*then correct your spellings here*
experience		
spectator		
allowed		
spontaneous		
possible		
delivered		
rewarded		
health		
legend		
unusual		
clumsy		
opposite		
available		
pianist		
attempt		
audience		
information		

Common Spelling Patterns, V8-V10

Even though students develop their vocabulary and learn spellings along the way, it is rare for them to categorise words according to spelling patterns.

However, an awareness of these issues will not only help them to remember spellings they have had difficulty with in the past, but it will also help them to learn and remember new spellings as their vocabulary continues to grow.

The following worksheets are therefore intended to allow students to explore this area for themselves and let their minds start to structure some of the patterns they recognise.

<u>V8</u> acts as an introduction to the topic, and is intended for you as the teacher to establish students' existing level before proceeding. This is an informal means of following the well-established 'test-teach-test' pattern and helps you to pitch your teaching at the level students are at: put another way, as I tell my CELTA observers, you cannot pitch a tent in mid-air.

One aspect that might need further explanation is the issue of silent letters: only 'b' is included in this worksheet, which deals with word endings, but you may also wish to elicit further silent letters which you would have expected your class to have come across, such as the 'k' in 'know' and the 'w' in 'write' etc.

Note also that the extension activity for V8 requires you to refer back to a reading text, preferably one you have done recently, which is likely to be full of examples of these patterns.

<u>V9</u> is based on specific vocabulary, although this is an activity which would be easy to replicate with your own list or with words your students have spelled incorrectly in their own written work.

<u>V10</u> could also be adapted to review other vocabulary, although this categorisation works particularly well here, as you might like to try and elicit how many syllables a word ending in 'ick' has compared to a word ending in 'ic'... and ask students to come up with some more words with these endings, or compare this rule with the spelling of one-syllable words which use other vowels.

V8   Introduction to Common Spelling Patterns

Look at these common word endings: these are some of the many spelling patterns used in the English language.

Can you think of one example for each word ending?

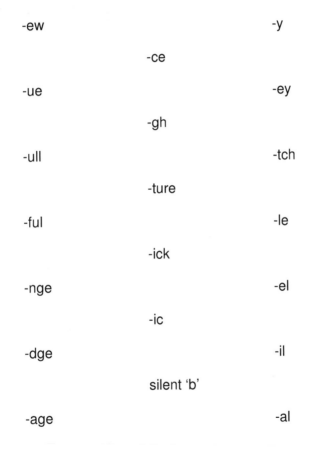

-ew

               -ce

-ue

               -gh

-ull

               -ture

-ful

               -ick

-nge

               -ic

-dge

               silent 'b'

-age

-y

-ey

-tch

-le

-el

-il

-al

Now look at your reading text. Notice how many words you can find which use these word endings. You can list the examples in the correct section above.

V9 Common Word Endings

Choose the correct ending for the beginning of the words in the box.

pock	swi	monk	sna	fri	electr
bas	clu	jock	i	turk	
jew	troll	terrif	wa	bull	energet
tunn	la	trav	scra	characterist	
we	mon	lo	lev	hon	knowle
tow	trag	bri	top	quarr	

List the words here.

    <u>-ey</u>   <u>-el</u>   <u>-et</u>

    <u>-ic</u>   <u>-dge</u>   <u>-tch</u>

How many of these words can you use in the same sentence?

V10 | 'c' and 'k' Endings

Can you make a word from each box by adding two letters, so that each word ends with either 'c' or 'k'?

mus		stu

ne		dri

What are these three common endings for words ending in 'c' or 'k'? Write them as headings for the columns below, and list each of the words above in the correct column.

1)_____.   2)_____.   3)_____.

All the words in the box have been mixed up. Work out the correct spellings, and then list each word in the right column above.

lcki	ckab	cmaks	cibplu	sniiiecctf
skitn	niclk	cklif	suimc	ikpc	kosc
kihnt	acinp	colk	ictsk	ctuaethni
kin	ickk	kinp	ekdc	nisk	kilbn

Now try to write a paragraph using as many of these words as possible.

More Spelling Patterns, V11-V15

The following worksheets continue to lead students through activities which prompt them to make their own discoveries, with the intention that this will help them remember their learning.

<u>V11</u> covers additional word endings, and challenges students to recognise anagrams which have the same two letters missing: a clue here if necessary is to find the months... (or seasons!)

<u>V12</u> is intended to show the role of 'y' in words where there is no other vowel: in the warm-up section there is only one box containing a y which has letters missing ('mummy') whereas the other boxes containing only consonants cannot be re-arranged into words. (This worksheet also covers pronunciation of a 'y' and includes the pronunciation of 'y' as in 'syllable'.)

<u>V13</u> continues with vowels and could additionally be used to tempt students to investigate whether any combination of two vowels can be used in English spellings (see also V20).

Some answers as follows (although others are possible):
1: museum - bird - station – follow - hungry
5: nervous - century - situation - people - picture - decide
remember - throat - doctor - scared - neighbour – pocket

Then follows a review of the spelling patterns introduced in V8 – V13, including the opportunity to cover additional vocabulary.

<u>V14</u> starts with a warm-up anagrams section, and the boxed anagrams below it all have the same missing letter: create an example to show on the board. The answers are as follows:
Box 1: 'c' i.e. church - coin - car - call - cloud etc
Box 2: 'o' - Box 3: 'i' - Box 4: 't' - Box 5: 'r'

<u>V15</u> should not be too daunting for the students once they have completed V14, and you could always offer them a list of the correct answers for matching the answers instead of deducing them. (Alternatively you could make an extra activity setting the challenge of two letters missing from each box...)
Box 1: 's' - Box 2: 'u' - Box 3: 'y' - Box 4: 'h'
Box 5: 'w' - Box 6: 'a' - Box 7: 'k'

V11 | Two Letters Missing

Can you make a word from each box by adding two letters at the end?

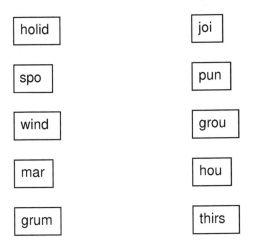

holid

joi

spo

pun

wind

grou

mar

hou

grum

thirs

Now look at the boxes below. All the spellings have been mixed up, and every box has the same last two letters missing. Can you work out which two letters are missing and write the correct spellings?

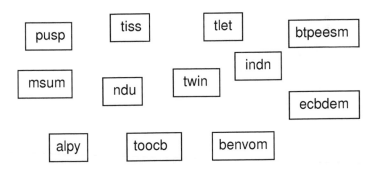

pusp

tiss

tlet

btpeesm

msum

ndu

twin

indn

ecbdem

alpy

toocb

benvom

Now try to write a sentence or a paragraph using as many of these words as possible.

V12 Y am I Special?

Some of the mixed up words in the boxes below have letters missing.
Circle the boxes where you think something is missing.

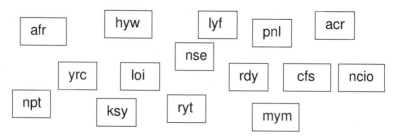

afr   hyw   lyf   pnl   acr

nse

yrc   loi   rdy   cfs   ncio

npt   ksy   ryt   mym

Which of the words above do not contain a vowel? How is that possible?

The letter 'y' can be pronounced in different ways. Work out the
correct spellings of the words below and then group them in the
columns below according to the pronunciation of the 'y'.

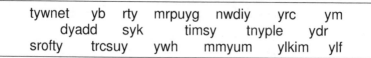

tywnet   yb   rty   mrpuyg   nwdiy   yrc   ym
dyadd   syk   timsy   tnyple   ydr
srofty   trcsuy   ywh   mmyum   ylkim   ylf

<u>like 'i' in Hi</u>   <u>like 'e' in me</u>

Can you think of any words with a 'y' which is pronounced in any
other way?
For example, what letters are missing in this word? s_ll_b_e

V13 | Missing Vowels

1 *There is a vowel missing from each of the mixed up words in the box below. Can you work out what these words are?*

mumus	dbr	nottis	wlolf	gnyhr

2 *The following mixed up words also have a vowel missing, but more than one answer is possible. How many words can you make by adding a vowel to these letters?*

kpr	rts	nrb	twh	sdh	htsr	wls

3 *Now look at this box. In each of these words, there are two different vowels missing: fill in the gaps, without using double letters. Again, sometimes more than one answer is possible.*

r___n   cl___d   h___d   cr___l   n___se   j___n

c___t   p___nt   gr___nd   l___d   appl___d

j___nt   tr___n   b___l   bl___   br___d   sh___t

w___rd   f___d   bel___ve   l___n   ___roplane

4 *In this box, all the vowels in each word are missing, but the letters have been kept in the correct order. Can you work out what all the words are?*

dctr	ktchn	brthdy	mprtnt	chldrn

5 *Now look at these mixed up words, which also have their vowels missing. Can you make a word by adding vowels to these letters? How many times can you make two or more answers? You can only add vowels to the word.*

nsvr	rtcyn	tnts	lpp	rptc	ddc
bmrmr	rtht	rdcs	nrhbg	kptc	

6 *When you have finished, make a quiz for your partner by writing some words without their vowels. If you want, you could also mix up the letters.*

The words in the box below are mixed up. Can you work out the correct spellings?

trta	kcro	igcrat	lknci	iphcn	aedrd
tojni	htca	nitks	tonpi	aetdnsi	knbil

The mixed up words in the following boxes all have a letter missing: in each box the same letter is missing from all of the words. Can you work out which letter is missing for the words in each box and then list all the correct spellings?

1

rhuhc   ion   ra
lal   ludo
hum   harm   abk
ikp   lbpui
eeembdr

2

krp   hsp
kcs
ldu   wc
emrebnv
wl   li

3

drb   hsd
blo
kkc   canp
pkn
ydnw   njo

4

rmso   unr   lla   nih   iwh   hta
cski   hsuo   onw   rltee   boorce

5

lig   kop   ikst   okf
uf   shu   awd
kap   heet   nuod   odwc
owg   yc   inend
otsfy   sdape

If you have finished, write sentences combining one word from each box.

In each of the boxes below, all of the mixed up words have the same letter missing. Can you work out which letter is missing for each box and then list all the correct spellings?

1
rift	torp	rbut
atr	afcr	
lmla	icph	ikc
nki	umeo	
won	bepmerte	etsir
enio	myit	

2
bnr	tyrdtsaa
hts	ncph
skct	icsm	to
mersm	dnre
cytsr	pmgry

3
naw	ewlol	rd	rt
eyrdstae	ummm	aer	
veah	neplt	lohl	lf

4
rist	soer	tru	re
atyudrs	ifs	lal	
nic	tne	nitk	
oesu	wo	yw	

5
as	alrc	aln
his	lsl	
nobr	odn	eyntt
bol	iwond	
los	irten	on

6
wj	rhsp	rf	rj
llf	kmsc	nwd	
yddd	deh	edr	drbe

7
yuert	arb	adr	ihnt	naht
ilc	cen	inrd	ys	ylmi

Suffixes, V16-V18

Suffixes follow on nicely from spellings of word endings, with an additional difference: the use of the suffix '-ful' for example, conveys meaning, in the same way as prefixes such as 'pre-', or 'over-', while other suffixes are most commonly used to form a noun, adjective or verb from another related word.

V16 is therefore an opportunity to lead students through the process of identifying common suffixes used for adjectives, and for you to gain an initial understanding of how much they know already.

V17 then leads on to various activities: for students to form nouns from adjectives, and to form both nouns and adjectives from verbs. Although it is not specified in the notes on the worksheet, you may also want to point out that we can commonly make a verb from a noun by using the ending '-ise' (or '-ize' in the USA) – for example 'standardise'.

V18 lists a suffixes challenge which you may want to adapt for differentiation within your class or alternatively break down into smaller chunks when photocopying it for the students. The list provides for a detailed review of suffixes and offers an opportunity to cover new vocabulary and categorise words.

From a practical point of view, it is worth noting that a whole-class feedback session for the full list would be very time-consuming, and that it would be better to collect students' work for checking, or hand out a photocopied list of answers. Alternatively you could split your answer sheet into sections, and give different answers to different groups within the class, so they could then check their work with each other.

As a further extension, students may notice that some of the items in the list are already words in themselves, and it would be a valuable vocabulary activity to set the task of checking which items are words and finding out their meanings.

For more advanced students, you could even go into a discussion of which of these words are related by meaning, and which merely exist as words by coincidence.

V16 | An Introduction to Suffixes

Can you match the start of these words with the correct suffix?

qualific	-ity
reli	-ition
compet	-ious
popular	-ability
suspic	-ation

Which of the words above is an adjective?

Think of some examples of words using the suffixes below until you can circle the suffixes which are used for adjectives.

-ation   -able   -ence   -ous   -ive   -ish

-ition   -ance   -ful   -ible   -ibility

-ness   -ity   -less   -ist   -ure   -ability

Often we form an adjective from a noun using a suffix. Look at the nouns below: can you form the appropriate adjectives? An example has been done for you. Take care with your spellings.

nature - *natural*	fame -	beauty -
fashion -	child -	nation -
wonder -	mystery -	logic -

V17 More Suffixes

Choose the correct suffix to make a new word from each of the words in the left-hand column. Take care with your spellings!

enjoy	-ity
suitable	-able
happy	-ation
qualify	-al
critic	-ness

Notice how suffixes can be used to make a noun from an adjective as well as an adjective from a noun. We also use suffixes to make an adjective or a noun from a verb.

Use a suffix to make nouns from the adjectives below.

Now make nouns from these verbs.

important	introduce
rare	type
elegant	exist
perfect	add
ambitious	decide
responsible	attract

Often we can make an adjective as well as a noun from the same verb:

	Adjective	Noun
accept		
rely		
create		
differ		
imagine		

Suffixes Challenge

Can you use a suffix to make a word from each of these beginnings?

posi	confu	happi
televi	exhibi	import
tour	practical	refer
excell	oppos	invisib
entr	actr	neighbour
journal	faithful	injec
expendit	transfu	fair
possib	educa	adapta
atten	abund	correspond
neglig	provi	ignor
ill	mother	retribu
national	opti	physic
inherit	fu	apprehen
qualifica	availab	expul
readi	interfer	ecolog
politi	dura	matern
quota	confess	occa
brother	waitr	circumfer
possess	exist	ven
hospital	conservation	applica
infin	prescript	anticipa
ambi	independ	trea
prema	sick	weightless
busi	inconveni	responsib
ident	solu	simplic
musi	mois	vul
experi	popula	technical
informa	appear	econom
flexib	disab	imbal
punc	transla	presenta
similar	acquaint	plea
nuis	abbrevia	intru
influ	wit	resid

You may now find it useful to list these words according to their suffix.

It must continually be emphasised that spelling work is never an end in itself but is of crucial importance in students' written work, when they can also use their knowledge of one word to help them spell another.

This worksheet attempts to demonstrate this to students by applying the use of spelling knowledge in contextualised sentences, and sets them a paragraph of writing so you can assess their application of spelling patterns in written work.

Question 1 does not specify that students need to attempt to fit rhyming words into the same sentences; note that this can be a supplementary challenge if the stronger students have finished 'too quickly' (!) – the intended answers are:
I put my numb thumb in the crumbs.
My friend found a round box on the ground.
It's true, he's put blue glue on the paper.

Question 2 could easily be adapted for students if they are likely to find it too hard: this needs to be done when you photocopy the worksheets, but a good example of differentiation would be to fill in the first word of each answer on the photocopies you plan to give to some students, and to write the target words in a separate box for weaker students if appropriate. The advantage of differentiation of this kind is that each student's final answer is the same and as a result there are no complications with the process of reviewing the answers with the whole class.

There are many other ways this worksheet could be used, including a pronunciation review, and a group activity listing other words using the same spelling patterns. Note that the same text is used again in G4 to highlight the use of articles, with an additional final paragraph.

Question 3 is likely to need you to have some clues ready for the students if they are to guess the missing words in the final sentence. I would write 'd', 'f', and 'w' on the board and if no one could guess the answer I would then use these letters to create anagrams of the three words as a final clue. Then students are ready to write their own paragraphs.

V19 Using Spelling Strategies

[1] *Can you fill in the gaps below using the words in this box?*

| blue crumbs found glue ground round numb thumb true |

I put my_____ _____ in the _____.

My friend _____ a _____ box on the _____.

It's _____, he's put _____ _____ on the paper.

[2] *Now try to fill in the gaps below using words with these spelling patterns.*

| -ough   -ight   -ought   -tion |

Fatima had a _____ and a sore throat so she_____ she should go to see her doctor. When she was a child, however, Fatima had to go to hospital for an _____ so she is scared of doctors.

She got nervous sitting in the waiting room so she started reading an article in a magazine about a country in Africa which was suffering from a severe _____ because there wasn't _____ rain for the crops. She realised how _____ life is for some people and she decided to look on the _____ side of her own situation.

The doctor was very kind and he gave her some chest _____. She was very happy and on her way home she saw a book shop near the _____ where she _____ a picture book for her children. It was very _____ so it was easy for her to carry and that _____ she read the book to her children.

[3] *Try to write another paragraph about Fatima, so that the story ends with the sentence below. Underline the words in your work which use a spelling pattern you have studied. Can you guess the missing words here?*

So he made a _____ that he would find a big _____ on his _____.

[4] *Can you make any more sentences like this which use three (or more!) words with the same spelling pattern?*

An Unofficial History of early Britain, V20

V20 Link to G20

This text may require you to pre-teach a certain amount of vocabulary but this does not all need to be done in one go.

One approach may be to photocopy the worksheet in three sections so that it appears less intimidating for the students, and to pre-teach the necessary vocabulary one stage at a time.

In addition, the worksheet may easily be differentiated by filling in gaps as appropriate for certain students before photocopying, particularly with names which students might not know.

Note again that a photocopied answer sheet would be more efficient than a whole-class feedback session with a worksheet of this length, and that this is provided by worksheet G20 which looks at use of the passive forms in the text. Once more, this could also be split up so that each group has one set of answers but still has to check the other answers with another group.

Even if you feel the content of the text is not applicable to your students, this worksheet would be very easy to replicate with any other article or reading material which students have used in class, and again this could easily be differentiated for different learners.

However, the article does bring up many potential further topics of study, including European country names and geography, the origin of our dating system, the original use of British pounds and pennies, and Macbeth, mentioned in his historical context.

Other applications could be for students to find out about the main events of British history since 1066, or to carry out further research about a place, person or event mentioned in the passage. Note that the text also gives some background about King Canute, who is fabled as the King who stood on the beach and tried to order the tide to go back.

Furthermore, when students have completed the work on passives in G20, they could also use this text as a template to help them write about the history of their own, or another, country.

Not a lot is known about the history of the Britain before 1066, when William the Conqueror famously invaded. The following has been taken from reputable sources but cannot be guaranteed as 100% accurate!

Can you fill in the correct vowels in order to read this history of Britain?

R_c_rds w_r_ k_pt by th_ R_m_ns, wh_ b_g_n th__r c_nq__st _f Br_t__n _n th_ y__r _D 43, c_pt_r_ng wh_t _s n_w C_lch_st_r _n th_ c__st __st _f L_nd_n. _ft_r _b__t 40 y__rs th_y h_d d_f__t_d th_ C_l_d_n__ns (wh_ l_v_d _n wh_t _s n_w Sc_tl_nd) _lth__gh _ft_r th_ y__r 180 th_y r_tr__t_d b_h_nd H_dr__n's W_ll.

D_r_ng th_ __rly 400's th_ R_m_ns _pp__r t_ h_v_ l_ft Br_t__n, _nd _t th_s t_m_ _th_r _nv_d_rs c_m_ t_ Br_t__n _sp_c__lly fr_m th_ _r__s _f __r_p_ wh_ch _r_ n_w kn_wn _s Sc_nd_n_v__ _nd G_rm_ny.

_nd_r R_m_n r_l_ Br_t__n h_d b_c_m_ str_ngly _nfl__nc_d by th_ Chr_st__n ch_rch, _nd s_m_ h_st_r__ns s_y th_t _n 525 th_ c_nc_pt _f _D _nd BC d_t_s w_s b_g_n wh_n th_ d_t_ _f th_ b_rth _f Chr_st w_s c_lc_l_t_d – _nd _n 604 St P__l's C_th_dr_l _n L_nd_n w_s f__nd_d.

Th_ _r_g_n _f Br_t_sh p__nds _nd p_nn__s _s th__ght t_ h_v_ b__n _n _D 747 wh_n K_ng _ff_ d_v_d_d _ p__nd-w__ght _f s_lv_r _nt_ 240 s_lv_r p_nn__s. L_t_r, _n 973, _ n_w c__n_g_ w_s _ntr_d_c_d by K_ng _dg_r, w_th th_ r_y_l p_rtr__t b_c_m_ng _ r_g_l_r f__t_r_ _n c__ns _t th_t t_m_.

Th_ _nd _f th_ 700's w_r_ th_ st_rt _f _ l_ng p_r__d _f _nv_s__ns by th_ V_k_ngs, w_th th_ D_n_sh t_k_ng c_ntr_l _f th_ n_rth _nd __st _f _ngl_nd _n _ tr__ty _f _D 880 w_th _lfr_d th_ Gr__t _f W_ss_x.

Th_ _ngl_sh h_d s_m_ s_cc_ss _g__nst th_ D_n_s _n th_ __rly 900's _ft_r K_ng _lfr_d's d__th, b_t th_r_ w_s _ r_n_w_d V_k_ng _ss__lt fr_m _D 980 _nw_rds _nd _n 1016 C_n_t_ pr_cl__m_d h_ms_lf K_ng _f D_nm_rk, N_rw_y _nd _ngl_nd.

_ft_r th_ d__th _f C_n_t_ _n 1035 M_cb_th _s r_ck_n_d t_ h_v_ t_k_n th_ thr_n_ _f Sc_tl_nd _n 1040, wh_l_ _dw_rd th_ C_nf_ss_r b_c_m_ K_ng _f _ngl_nd s__n _ft_rw_rds _nd th_ b__ld_ng _f L_nd_n's W_stm_nst_r _bb_y st_rt_d _n 1052.

Wh_n H_r_ld II b_c_m_ K_ng _n J_n__ry 1066 _t w_s th_ N_rw_g__ns wh_ _nv_d_d, b_t _ft_r h_s f_rc_s w_r_ w__k_n_d _n s_cc_ssf_lly d_f_nd_ng th_ _ngl_sh fr_m th_t _tt_ck, D_k_ W_ll__m _f N_rm_ndy th_n _nv_d_d _t H_st_ngs n__r th_ _nd _f th_ y__r.

Learning New Vocabulary, V21-V22

V21 is intended as another mechanism to lead students into more in-depth self-study, and to help them recognise that there are endless possibilities for extending their vocabulary.

First of all, students put the words in alphabetical order and then find them in an English-English dictionary. It may be worth planning some lesson time around the topic of using a dictionary in order to show what information is provided with each definition, and also to highlight the possibility that many different meanings may be listed for the same word.

Having listed the definitions which they feel will be most useful, students then write sentences for each word: this is a very important concept checking stage where you are able to assess in context whether they have used their words correctly.

If you encourage students to carry out this activity regularly, they will be able to build up their vocabulary in an authentic manner, with the encouragement that you are checking their work is correct. You may also be able to incorporate a review of these words into future classes when most applicable.

As well as the worksheet opposite there is a 'refill' page overleaf, with strips of words which can be photocopied for additional practice or to meet the right level for your students. As an additional, but difficult, activity, you could also set students the task of writing their own definition for a common word and then comparing it with the dictionary entry.

V22 is intended to help students learn vocabulary in context instead of an abstract vacuum, as this is likely to help them remember the new words. This is a similar technique to personalisation, which can be employed with any words you need to cover in your classes. Note also that by making students focus on the construction of the gapfill sentences they will develop skills for recognising when a verb, noun, adjective, or adverb is needed, thus also helping them with their own writing.

V21 | New Vocabulary is everywhere

Every student needs to be able to learn new vocabulary from reading a book or a newspaper. Look at the words below which are examples of words you might find in an article.

1 *Put the words in alphabetical order by writing the numbers 1-8 next to the words.*

Number   Definition

irritating

perceive

spine

venture

series

eclectic

vested

election

2 *Use an English dictionary to find the meaning of the words. Notice that some words have more than one meaning: next to the list above, write down the definitions that you think will be most useful for you.*

3 *Now, on the back of this page, try to write a sentence for each word.*

4 *Can you use all these words in one paragraph which links them together with a realistic meaning?*

mankind	secondary
majority	pedestrian
childhood	online
fist	novel
forensic	qualification
portable	statue
terrified	quotation
nearby	probable

splutter	slogan
silicon	brochure
quadruple	leaflet
redundancy	mature
successor	proverb
technological	catalogue
artificial	literature
queue	source

V22 | Vocabulary Gapfills

Look at the sentences below. Which gaps need a verb? – a noun? – or an adjective?
Can you complete each sentence with one of the words on the right?

1. I was very _____ that I had the best teacher in the school.

2. I think English is the best way to _____ with people from another country.

3. Jane's _____ was always to go to university.

4. I'm so sorry I'm late! It didn't _____ to me that you'd be waiting for me.

5. It is hard to read instructions if they are _____.

6. I think electricity is the greatest _____ in the world.

7. My mum was worried when I lost my _____.

8. The woman we met used to be a _____ business manager in London.

ambition

invention

appetite

complicated

communicate

fortunate

prominent

occur

When you have finished, try to write another sentence using each of these words.

Dictionary Treasure, V23

This game works really well as students self-adapt it to their own level, and learn new words in the process. You need to make sure you have enough English-English dictionaries to go around, and then set students on task in pairs, or small groups – ideally of no more than four, otherwise some of the students may use it as an excuse not to involve themselves fully.

First of all the students have to flick through their dictionaries looking for suitable words, and even though they might think at first that they will not be able to find any, they will soon realise that there are more than enough words to choose from.

Once they have listed at least three words in each category, reinforcing their own learning, they then choose one word with each suffix and write it on the back of their page along with the definition: each group should be making a list of nine words.

If you choose to explain the game in advance, they will also understand the relevance of the extension work here, which is to list more difficult words that they can find, along with their definitions: you are going to collect the worksheets when everyone is ready and use the definitions listed by the students to play a game as follows.

You will read out the definition of a word and students have to guess the word you are defining. This can be adapted into an individual spelling test format if you prefer, although I like to play it as a team game where the pairs or groups work together with each question. You could also match up pairs at this stage into teams of four if appropriate.

My way of doing it is to make each team write down every word you define, but go round the class so the teams each answer a question in turn; if the team whose turn it is gets it wrong, you can pass it on to the next team for a bonus point until one team gets it right... etc!

I like to make it fun, and keep the scores for each team on the board – but I would also revisit the most relevant words in another lesson to reinforce the learning that is taking place.

V23 | Dictionary Treasure

Find at least three words from the dictionary using these suffixes.

-ance e.g. acceptance

1.   2.   3.

-ence e.g. difference

1.   2.   3.

-tion e.g. introduction

1.   2.   3.

-sion e.g. decision

1.   2.   3.

-ist e.g. typist

1.   2.   3.

-ure e.g. pleasure

1.   2.   3.

-ness e.g. happiness

1.   2.   3.

-bility e.g. reliability

1.   2.   3.

-ity e.g. popularity

1.   2.   3.

Now choose one word from each category and on the back of this page write down the meaning given in the dictionary for each word.

If you have time you can also try to find some more difficult new words from the dictionary and write down these words and their definitions.

Idiomatic Expressions, V24

Idiomatic expressions provide a lot of richness in a language, and students always like to learn them because they have similar expressions of their own: if you are working with a monolingual group try to teach English equivalents of phrases they already use in their own language.

This activity can be photocopied into three parts, not so much because the gapfill exercise is intimidating, but because the feedback stage could be quite time-consuming if you try to explain the meaning of all the expressions in one go.

Depending on the level of your students, you may decide that a handful of new expressions is enough at any one time, but the key thing is to provide a context for any new language like this so that it has a peg to hang on in their learning.

One way to reinforce these expressions, however, would be to prepare dictation sentences using the new language, and once you have checked their work, ask your students in pairs to discuss possible contexts where these sentences may be used: for example students could write out conversation dialogues using the expressions they have learned, and this may also lead into a good opportunity to explain the issue of not causing offence in a situation where they need to be polite.

You may also be able to use these expressions in conjunction with other material which you have already covered in class, especially a speaking or reading task.

If you do find that your students enjoy vocabulary like this, it can be a very useful way to lead into a review of other skills such as sentence construction: for example you could make a gapfill activity with the main aim of highlighting which gaps need a noun, verb, adjective, or adverb etc, and include idiomatic expressions with gaps as a part of the review.

One of the great skills of review and consolidation is to dress up the same learning aim in so many different ways over the course of your lessons that students don't even realise they have been covering the same objective all along...!

V24 | Idiomatic Expressions

Choose the correct missing word in the following common English expressions. Can you guess what they mean?

Part 1: the body

before your very_____.	head
to_____up to something.	teeth
to be_____deep in something.	eyes
not able to make_____or tail of something.	face
to pull someone's_____.	knee
to be fed up to the back_____.	leg

Part 2: animals

to have a_____in your bonnet.	fish
to be a book_____.	cat
to let the_____out of the bag.	rat
like a_____out of water.	bee
be a_____on the wall.	sheep
the_____race.	fly
the black_____of the family.	worm

Part 3: various

to _____on thin ice.	middle
to hit the_____on the head.	breath
to be_____for something.	downhill
to make a_____and dance about it.	kick
to be_____and dry.	touch
something has gone_____.	dying
to be in the_____of nowhere.	sailing
to_____up a fuss.	walk
I wouldn't_____it with a bargepole!	fuse
to be a_____of fresh air.	nail
something isn't all plain_____.	home
to be on a short_____.	song

Grammar Reviews, G1-G4

Students always like to learn grammar as they feel they are learning for 'real'. However, they do not always realise that they have only 'learnt' grammar when they can use it correctly in their spoken and written English. A particular grammar point can be repeated on a worksheet until the answers are easy, and predictable... but this means nothing until the student can master the same issue in their own writing, in a free context. Hence these and all grammar activities need to be continually related back to students' own work and their authentic mistakes.

G1 is a review of the differences between adjectives and adverbs, and includes an opportunity to remind students when they should use an article before an adjective, i.e. when it is referring to a noun: no matter how easily they can do this in a class situation this is a key mistake that my students continue to make in their written work and needs regular reinforcement.

Question 3 also allows you to recap irregular adverbs such as 'good'-'well' and the usage of 'nearly'. Note that Question 4 may need clear explanation, with an example shown on the board.

G2 covers word order in sentences using adjective and adverbs, with G2b designed as a differentiated version to check students' ability to choose between an adjective or an adverb.

G3 is provided so that it is not necessary to carry out a long class review of all the answers, but this worksheet can then be used in various additional ways. For example, I would set the task of extending each of the sentences with a linking word, and when the stronger students have finished that, ask them to add at least one adjective and one adverb to each sentence.

Be careful also when students set quiz questions for each other: you need to monitor carefully to ensure the sentences they make are correct *before* they mix up the word orders (!)

G4 reviews the use of articles, linking with spelling pattern work.

G1 | Adjectives and Adverbs

1 *Can you match the beginning and end of these sentences?*

I drove	old
My car is	newest
It is a	faster than mine
My friend's car is	red car
His car is the	quickly

2 *Which sentence has a word missing?*

It is beautiful.   It is beautiful car.

3 *Look at the sentences below and correct the mistakes.*

I ran quicker to a bus stop. _____.

The Grand Hotel is nearly here. _____.

He is a really well teacher. _____.

Mars is biggest than Venus. _____.

4 *Now look at the words below. Choose which words fit together best and write sentences using the adjectives and adverbs correctly.*

quiet   neat   careful   students   speaks   stands up

quietly   neatly   carefully   drivers   clothes   writes

| G2a | Adjective and Adverb Sentences |

Can you put the words in the right order to make correct sentences?

1 school is our popular

2 popular a is school it

3 very old is University Oxford.

4 very old has university a Oxford.

5 very London is expensive.

6 place house expensive to an London buy is a.

7 slowly friend my walks.

8 in the some very students speak class quietly.

9 often quiet write the very quickly students.

10 clearly exams need in to your you write.

11 any not be to spelling make careful mistakes.

When you have finished, practise speaking with your partner using sentences of your own which include adjectives and adverbs.

G2b | Adjective and Adverb Sentences

Can you put the words in the right order? You need to choose one of the options from each box to complete each sentence.

1. school is our | popular   poppullar

2. a is school it. | popular   poppullar

3. very is University Oxford. | old   older

4. very has university a Oxford. | old   older

5. very London is. | expennsive   expensive

6. place house to an London buy is a. | expennsive   expensive

7. friend my walks. | slow   slowly

8. in the some very students speak class. | quiet   quietly

9. often write the very quickly students. | quiet   quietly

10. exams need in to your you write. | clear   clearly

11. any not be to spelling make mistakes. | careful   carefully

Now write some sentences of your own using adjectives and adverbs.

G3 Adjective and Adverb Sentences Continued

Check the correct sentences here.

☐ 1 Our school is popular.

☐ 2 It is a popular school.

☐ 3 Oxford University is very old.

☐ 4 Oxford has a very old university.

☐ 5 London is very expensive.

☐ 6 London is an expensive place to buy a house.

☐ 7 My friend walks slowly.

☐ 8 Some students in the class speak very quietly.

☐ 9 The quiet students often write very quickly.

☐ 10 You need to write clearly in your exams.

☐ 11 Be careful not to make any spelling mistakes.

*Now can you think of some more sentences using adjectives and adverbs?
First write the sentences in full, and then mix the words up on another
piece of paper to give to your partner as a quiz.*

*For example, if you write the sentence 'I have got a blue pen',
you can mix the words up like this:*

pen   blue   got   I   a   have

and then give it to your partner.

Try to make at least five sentences like this, using adjectives and adverbs.

G4 | Using Articles

Can you fill in the gaps below using a, an, the, or nothing (–)?

My friend found _____ round box on _____ ground.

He made _____ wish that he would find _____ big fish on his dish.

It's true, he's put _____ blue glue on _____ paper.

I put my numb thumb in _____ crumbs.

Now fill in the gaps in this story using a, an, the, or nothing (–).

Fatima had_____ cough and _____ sore throat so she thought she
should go to see her doctor. When she was _____ child, however,
Fatima had to go to _____ hospital for _____ operation so she is
scared of _____ doctors.

She got nervous sitting in _____ waiting room so she started
reading _____ article in _____ magazine about _____ country
in _____ Africa which was suffering from _____ severe drought
because there wasn't enough rain for _____ crops. She realised how
tough _____ life is for _____ some people and she decided to look
on _____ bright side of her own situation.

_____ doctor was very kind and he gave her _____ some chest
lotion. She was very happy and on her way home she saw _____ book
shop near _____ station where she bought _____ picture book for her
children. It was very light so it was easy for her to carry and that night
she read _____ book to her children.

_____ book was _____ story about _____ boy who didn't like
eating _____ vegetables, but if he made _____ wish when his mother
wasn't looking, he could change _____ vegetables on his plate into _____
different kind of _____ food. Fatima's children enjoyed _____ story.
_____ next day, however, Fatima's son said he didn't want to eat his
vegetables. Fatima told him he should be grateful that they had any
_____ food to eat at all, and she walked away to do _____ washing-
up, but he remembered _____ boy in _____ story. So he made
_____ wish that he would find _____ big fish on his dish.

Discuss with a partner: what would you wish for if you were that boy?

Verb Constructions, G5-G8

G5 is designed not merely as a test but as a first stage in showing students the three types of irregular past participle. I like to give students the task of grouping the participles with a colour system: choose colours that your students can either write or highlight with. Group 1 can be filled in with one colour, i.e. 'cut'-'cut'-'cut' and others with the same pattern. Group 2 will be words where the past participle is the same as the past simple, e.g. 'buy'-'bought'-'bought' and Group 3 will be the completely irregular ones. You could also use flashcards in these colours and highlight participles when they come up in reading texts. This colour system will help students to consolidate their groupings, and as they continue to come across other verbs you can encourage them to categorise them accordingly.

G6 is a review of the usage of either present perfect or past simple depending whether the time of the event is stated or not. A differentiated worksheet G6b is included to demonstrate an example of how the same material can be covered simultaneously by different students within the group.

G7 reviews 'for' and 'since' and also refers to the difference between 'been' and 'gone' when used as the past participle of 'go'. Question 2 also allows students to explore the usage of 'for' with both the present perfect and the past simple.

G8 then looks at constructions of verbs when used together. Students need to be able to use modal verbs without an 's' in the third person, and the worksheet is designed to show how different verbs are used together.

Students thus categorise a selection of verbs according to whether they need to be followed by an infinitive or an '-ing' form when used with another verb: the 'neither' column is for modal verbs, which (with the exception of 'ought') are followed by an infinitive without 'to'.

If students are not familiar with this vocabulary, let them read from an appropriate text to find the answers by discovery. Again, students can also continue to categorise new vocabulary in this way when they encounter it.

Can you fill in the past tense and past participles of all these verbs?

become		
begin		
buy		
choose		
come		
cut		
do		
drink		
drive		
eat		
fly		
forget		
get		
give		
have		
keep		
let		
lose		
make		
put		
run		
say		
see		
sleep		
speak		
stand		
take		
tell		
think		
write		

When you have finished, use a colour or highlighter pen to group them.

G6a | Introduction to Present Perfect

1 *Which word is correct? Underline your answer.*

Have you ever (speak / speaked / spoke / spoken) to Mr. Sykes?

He has never (give / gived / gave / given) me a birthday present!

2 *Can you fill in the correct form of the verb in brackets?*

a I _____ a letter to my friend last week. (write)

b My friend _____ to Brazil and Kenya. (go)

c I _____ my homework yet. (do)

Now choose the right verb by yourself and complete these sentences.

3 I _____ breakfast already.

4 We _____ tennis yesterday.

5 I'm sorry, I _____ to bring my books to school today.

6 _____ you ever _____ to Iranian music?

7 She _____ skiing last year.

8 I _____ my car, look how shiny it is!

9 _____ you _____ chicken for dinner last night?

10 They _____ never _____ my house.

11 I _____ my friend in Canada last night.

12 I _____ karaoke in a foreign language. Have you?

If you have finished, think of some more questions to ask your partner.

G6b | Introduction to Present Perfect

1 *Which word is correct? Underline your answer.*

Have you ever (speak / speaked / spoke / spoken) to Mr. Sykes?

He has never (give / gived / gave / given) me a birthday present!

2 *Can you fill in the correct form of the verb in brackets?*

a I _____ a letter to my friend last week. (write)

b My friend _____ to Brazil and Kenya. (go)

c I _____ my homework yet. (do)

Now choose a verb from the box below to complete these sentences.

3 I _____ breakfast already.

4 We _____ tennis yesterday.

5 I'm sorry, I _____ to bring my books to school today.

6 _____ you ever _____ to Iranian music?

7 She _____ skiing last year.

8 I _____ my car, look how shiny it is!

9 _____ you _____ chicken for dinner last night?

10 They _____ never _____ my house.

11 I _____ my friend in Canada last night.

12 I _____ karaoke in a foreign language. Have you?

forget	listen	clean	eat	visit
play	call	sing	go	have

If you have finished, think of some more questions to ask your partner.

G7   Present Perfect Review

1 *Can you match each question with the appropriate reply, and put the words in order to make the correct answer?*

Is this your house?	Kelly been have married Mr Mrs 1968 since and
Which couple have been married the longest?	seven half no been since here I've past.
Have you just arrived?	lived here since I old seven I've was yes years
How long have you known Ann?	school at since together were we

2 *Can you fill in the gaps in these sentences?*

I have never _____ to Australia.

Where's John at the moment? Oh, he's not here – he's _____ to the canteen.

I don't want to leave this school. I _____ here for five years.

I enjoyed school too. I have left now but I _____ there for three years.

3 *Now fill in the gaps below and add some more sentences to the dialogue.*

How many hours have you _____ this week?

Not enough! My baby has _____ me awake every night!

Babies are so beautiful!

Yes, but he has _____ before 6am every morning and his baby clothes have _____ us a fortune already!

G8 | Using Verbs: to –ing or not to –ing?

Circle the words below which do not use an 's' in the present tense for he, she, or it. These verbs are called modal verbs.

decide   enjoy   start   can   should

    might   finish   want   seem

need   expect   must   refuse   could

    would   may   forget   arrange

When we are joining two verbs together, the second verb usually needs to be in the 'to' form or the '–ing' form. Can you make sentences using the verbs in the box and list the verbs in the correct columns below?

hope	finish	want	ought	can	enjoy
afford	might	avoid	give up	remember	
promise	learn	consider	fail	would	admit
agree	should	mention	attempt	imagine	

    <u>'to'</u>   <u>'–ing'</u>   <u>neither</u>

If you have finished, try to make sentences using the expression "I am looking forward to…" What is different about this construction?

Pre-intermediate Grammar, G9-G11

G9 is a review of relative clauses which is designed to lead students through different review stages into the production of written sentences. Question 1 covers 'who' and 'which' while Question 2 reviews other words often used in relative clauses.

The purpose of Questions 3 and 4 is to show the importance of getting the sentence right to avoid either confusion or the wrong meaning – and Questions 5 and 6 should allow the student to demonstrate their understanding.

G10 reviews the usage of past continuous in the context of a past tense event while something else was happening; note that all the verbs to be changed are given in the present tense.

In the 'during the day' game students will need to work in groups of about four with a pair of dice for each group. This game can also be played in smaller classes as an 'alibi' game where the teacher is a detective investigating a crime: for this version you may wish to allow students to note down any dice rolls they make which have already been filled in by someone else. After sufficient time for the students to have filled in some of the gaps on their worksheets, the teacher announces that anyone without an alibi for a certain time will be called in for questioning. In this way bring a group of students to the front and 'interrogate' them with grammar questions. A right answer allows them to return to their group 'innocent' but anyone who answers incorrectly is 'guilty'!

G11 reviews question forms in a variety of past tenses. First of all the students work in pairs to deduce the correct word order of the questions in the present tense column, and then they have to work out which word is represented by a * in the past tense column in order to form these questions correctly.

The activity reviews word order in questions as well as the form and meaning of different past tenses. In the extension work note that the important element is that students ask their partner questions, even if they do not form present and past equivalents. Take care, however, to monitor that students do not simply use present and past simple: ensure that they stretch themselves by using the tenses you have been teaching in class recently.

G9   Relative Clauses

1 *What words would you use to join the following sentences together?*

He's got a new girlfriend. She works in a garage.
Here's an article. It might interest you.

2 *Now match the following sentence halves together.*

Here's the book	when I first met you.
I saw that man	where I can find sandals?
Do you know a shop	whose car crashed last week.
I'll always remember the day	that you were looking for.

3 *How would you join these sentences together?*

Students live next door. They keep playing loud music.
The room has got a big table. It is my mum's kitchen.
The key opens the garage. It is kept above the sink.

4 *What is the difference between these two sentences?*

The girl likes the cat that has black hair.
The girl that has black hair likes the cat.

5 *Now fill in the missing words in this conversation:*

I know a girl_____dad is in prison.

Is that the big prison_____famous people are kept?

Yes! Her dad was sent there _____ Killer Joe was released.

I saw that on TV! I know the man _____ picked him up in the car!

6 *Finally, try and use all the words in this box to write a paragraph using as many relative clauses as you can.*

chair	who	CD	which	shop	that
man	when	pen	where	car	whose

Past Continuous

Make sentences from the words below, using the past continuous tense.

drive --- see a police car: *While I was driving, I saw a police car.*
wait --- have a coffee.
make a cake --- hear a noise.
watch TV --- start reading the newspaper.

Now can you match together the sentence halves in the columns below? Then write correct sentences by changing the verb tenses to either past continuous or past simple.

<he> walks home   it starts raining.

<they> play golf   his friend calls him.

<he> does his homework   there is a power cut.

<they> watch TV   a driver stops to ask him directions.

During the day yesterday
You will need two dice in each group to play this game. Roll the dice, and write a sentence about what you were doing at that time yesterday (unless someone else has already filled in what they were doing at the same time.) The winner is the person with the most sentences at the end of the game.

Dice Roll   Name   Your sentence

9 _____ at 9 o'clock yesterday.
10 _____ at 10 am yesterday.
11 _____.
12 _____ at 12 o'clock yesterday.
2 _____ at 2 pm yesterday.
3 _____.
4 _____.
5 _____.
6 _____.
7 _____.
8 _____.

G11 Questions in the Past and Present

*Put the words in order in both columns below to make questions to ask your partner. The questions in the second column use the same verb as the first column, but these are marked with * because you have to change them to the past tense.*

PRESENT TENSE		PAST TENSE
is day what it today	1	yesterday it what day *
teacher languages can speak your 3	2	speak 1999 teacher how your many in languages *
play you tennis with going to us are	3	before it going play you tennis raining started to *
you TV at watching the moment are	4	while did dinner eat you your TV watching you *
spoken you French ever have	5	before went school you French you spoken to *

Now make new questions for your partner in the present and past

1

2

3

Intermediate Grammar, G12-G16

It is important for students to have a good grasp of phrasal verbs and conditionals: they are so common in English that learners will have come across them long before they specifically study them in class.

G12 provides an opportunity for students to extend their phrasal verb vocabulary, and to show that some combinations of words do not exist. (You may want to consider covering this worksheet in two parts if much of it will be new for your group, so as to avoid getting bogged down in too many definitions.)

The answers for each of the boxes are:
1: 'up' i.e. bring up - hang up - set up etc
2: 'down' - 3: 'in' - 4: 'out' - 5: 'over' - 6: 'off'

G13 requires students to put the second half of the sentences in order and then match sentence halves together. The activity then leads in to an explanation or review of the possibility of an object splitting a phrasal verb up (i.e. another way of saying 'splitting up a phrasal verb'!). It is a fun extension activity for students to write their own phrasal verb sentences and chop them in half in the same way to set a quiz for their partner.

G14 is a similar activity including some intransitive phrasal verbs, and can be used to highlight the word order of object pronouns such as 'it' and 'them' (when used with verbs where a noun object could be used either before or after the preposition particle). Students can re-write these sentences with a noun object that makes sense, and work out the grammatical rule.

G15 models the target grammar in the True or False section, and then introduces the students to Murphy's Law, that things always go wrong! Depending on your students' level, they might enjoy thinking of other ideas along these lines.

G16 contrasts first and second conditional, firstly by relating to the students' own situation in the warm-up, and then referring back to these possible events in Question 4. By this stage students have been led through a check on the correct use of conditional tenses with the class feedback for Questions 2 and 3.

G12 | Phrasal Verbs

The mixed up words in each box are all words that can be used in phrasal verbs. Can you work out the correct spellings and then choose which one of these prepositions fits with every word in the box to make a phrasal verb?

up   down   over   in   off   out

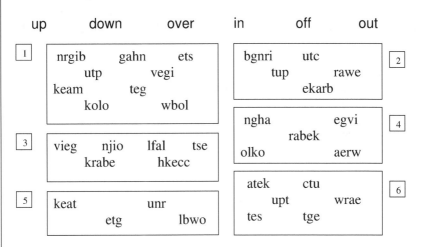

1
nrgib   gahn   ets
    utp   vegi
keam   teg
    kolo   wbol

2
bgnri   utc
        tup   rawe
            ekarb

4
ngha   egvi
        rabek
olko   aerw

3
vieg   njio   lfal   tse
    krabe   hkecc

6
atek   ctu
    upt   wrae
tes   tge

5
keat   unr
        etg   lbwo

Now choose a word from each box and write a sentence using a phrasal verb. How many tenses can you use in your six sentences?

up_____.

down_____.

over_____.

in_____.

off _____.

out_____.

Can you put the words in order and match the sentence halves together?

1

My sister gives	car up main another road the on!
Please look	computer yesterday my up.
I set	in up words a new the dictionary.
One of my friends cut	your up friend with?
When did you make	chocolates every up January.

2

He needs to cut	the ill because it cat so was down.
This strike might bring	bus off the supermarket the at 207.
I always get	company month over next the.
They had to put	his on down smoking.
An investor is going to take	government the down.

3

Someone always brings	cables over the.
Don't you want to join	around noise the with up all here?
Be careful not to trip	for leaflets cinema the out.
How do you put	games in the with?
I saw a man giving	parking the up problem.

Matching More Phrasal Verbs

Can you put the words in order and match the sentence halves together?

1

I set   when tunnel train off in a was the.

Sorry I'm late – I broke   pay up you it rise get a before!

Please can you hang   morning 7.30 this at off.

Sorry! I got cut   call I'm because a up expecting.

Don't give   the on here down way.

2

The plane didn't take   yesterday off.

She's going to blow   not if her you're over careful!

I'm going to set   the at out football club.

My brother always hangs   birthday her up them for party.

Slow down! You'll run   next up it week.

3

You need to look   do down, that again I won't.

It's OK now! Calm   until the off last it minute.

We need to check   you crossing are when the out road.

You always put   room leave out them you when the!

Remember to turn   them have we before lunch in.

G15 | Zero Conditional

1 *True or False?*

If you mix blue and yellow, you get green.
If you're in an accident, it's always the other person's fault.
If the temperature falls below zero, water freezes.

2 *Can you match these rules from Murphy's Law?*

If something begins well	you're probably wrong.
If you've got a job to do	you usually make it worse.
If you want to buy something	it often ends badly.
If you're absolutely sure about something	they usually don't make it any more.
If you try to make a difficult situation better	it always takes longer than you think.

3 *Now complete the sentences below.*

If you mix red and blue, _____.

_____ snows for several hours, _____.

_____ an egg on the floor, _____.

4 *Telling someone what to do. Use your own ideas to fill in the gaps.*

If it's raining, take a coat.

If you go walking today, _____.

_____ snow on the roads, _____ .

5 *Now write some more sentences like this with your own ideas.*

G16 First and Second Conditional

1 *Put the following events in order of likelihood when you leave class. Write 1) next to the most likely and 4) next to the least likely. Then compare your ideas with your partner.*

find an envelope full of money   send a text message to a friend

go to a shop on the way home   see an accident

2 *Can you match these sentence halves together?*

If I go to the museum,   I would need to have a shower.

If I went to America,   I will need to arrive early to set up.

If I played tennis tomorrow,   I will look around for a few hours.

If I play at the concert,   I would stay for at least a week.

3 *Which of the words in brackets would you choose in the sentences below? Then complete the sentences with your own ideas.*

If I < buy / bought > a new car, _____

_____.

If someone <calls / called > me tonight, _____

_____.

4 *Next, go back to the things at the top of the page which might happen after class. Make sentences in the correct tense using 'if'.*

If _____.

If _____.

If _____.

If _____.

5 *Now practise speaking with your partner in 'if' sentences about things that might happen this week.*

Elementary sentence construction needs to focus very much on the subject-plus-verb pattern of English, and only once this has been drummed into learners can you build any further. Yet now the passive, as with many grammar rules, means shamelessly introducing exceptions to rules you have taught so strictly...

G17 reviews the concept of direct objects for students who are already clear about the grammatical term 'subject'. You can also review other topics within the same worksheet by specifying, for example, that students must use an adjective, adverb, or specific words or tenses in each of their written sentences.

G18 then leads students through a review of indirect objects, e.g. 'run to the post office' (note that the number of verbs using a direct object here is zero) and intransitive verbs: note that all of the verbs listed at the top of the page are intransitive (in general usage – but you can always get caught out, e.g. 'running a car'!)

G19 builds further by reviewing the structure and meaning of the passive form, and also refers back to the work on direct objects as an extension. Question 1 highlights use of the word 'by' to show the agent of the passive verb, and Question 2 introduces the concept of changing the tense of the auxiliary 'to be'.

Question 3 then considers the issue of when it is not necessary to include the agent of a passive sentence. One of the prime uses of the passive is in fact when it is not known who carried out a certain action, for example in news bulletins, and this is worth pointing out to students at this stage. (A fun option here is to design a radio news activity, with your students as newsreaders.)

Question 4 then highlights the fact that a sentence using an intransitive verb cannot be changed into a passive form: e.g. the sentence 'The boy ran away this morning'.

G20 also brings out the point that passives are often used in authentic texts when the writer does not know (or, sometimes, does not want to say) who has carried out the action of a verb.

G21 then combines the use of the passive with phrasal verbs.

G17 | Direct Objects

Not only do verbs have a subject, who (or which) is 'doing' the verb, they often specifically refer to something that is being done. Can you match these verbs with their direct objects?

write   a cake
clean   an email
do   the car
buy   the washing

Now write sentences using these phrases. Try to use positive and negative forms, and extend your sentences with linking words.

1 _____
   _____.

2 _____
   _____.

3 _____
   _____.

4 _____
   _____.

Now try to write sentences using these verbs with a direct object:

make   speak   play   cook   use

Can you think of any other verbs which often use a direct object?

G18 | Indirect Objects and Intransitive Verbs

Sometimes the meaning of a verb can be complete without a direct object. Can you find the best way to match the two halves of each phrase? How many of these verbs use a direct object?

go away   to the post office
sleep   about the weather
run   for a week
complain   until 11 o'clock.

Which of the verbs use an indirect object? Now write sentences using these phrases with positive and negative forms, and linking words.

1 _____
_____ .

2 _____
_____ .

3 _____
_____ .

4 _____
_____ .

Look at the following sentences. Which one uses a direct object?

He stopped the car at the traffic lights.
He stopped at the traffic lights.

A verb that does not need a direct object is called an intransitive verb. Can you think of any other words like 'stop' in the example above, which are sometimes transitive and sometimes intransitive?

G19 Using Direct Objects to Start Passive Sentences

1 *When a verb has a direct object, it is possible to change the sentence to a passive form so that the object is referred to first. For example:*

Tom wrote the letter yesterday.
The letter was written by Tom yesterday.

These sentences have the same meaning. What differences are there?

2 *Now look at the sentences below. Work with a partner to change them into a passive form.*

My husband cooked the meal.

Many people used the train service.

Commuters buy newspapers every day.

How are passives formed in a different tense? Try to change one of the sentences above into future tense, and one into present perfect.

3 *Next, look at these sentences. Do they have the same meaning?*

Someone found a coat last week.
A coat was found last week.

4 *Match the sentence halves below. Can they be changed into passives?*

My brother built our	away this morning.
Someone is going to	borrowed our chairs.
The boy ran	the match in semi-darkness.
The driver parked the white	play our piano in the concert.
The teams finished	garden shed.
Our neighbours have	car under a bridge.

5 *Now look at the sentences you wrote on your G17 worksheet practising direct objects. Can you re-write all of those sentences using passives?*

G20 | Passives in Context

*Not a lot is known about the history of the Britain before 1066, when
William the Conqueror famously invaded. The following has been taken
from reputable sources but cannot be guaranteed as 100% accurate!*

Can you find how many times the passive forms of verbs have been used?

Records were kept by the Romans, who began their conquest of Britain in the
year AD 43, capturing what is now Colchester on the coast east of London. After
about 40 years they had defeated the Caledonians (who lived in what is now
Scotland) although after the year 180 they retreated behind Hadrian's Wall.

During the early 400's the Romans appear to have left Britain, and at this time
other invaders came to Britain especially from the areas of Europe which are now
known as Scandinavia and Germany.

Under Roman rule Britain had become strongly influenced by the Christian
church, and some historians say that in 525 the concept of AD and BC dates was
begun when the date of the birth of Christ was calculated – and in 604 St Paul's
Cathedral in London was founded.

The origin of British pounds and pennies is thought to have been in AD 747
when King Offa divided a pound-weight of silver into 240 silver pennies. Later, in
973, a new coinage was introduced by King Edgar, with the royal portrait
becoming a regular feature on coins at that time.

The end of the 700's were the start of a long period of invasions by the Vikings,
with the Danish taking control of the north and east of England in a treaty of AD
880 with Alfred the Great of Wessex.

The English had further success against the Danes in the early 900's after King
Alfred's death, but there was a renewed Viking assault from AD 980 onwards and
in 1016 Canute proclaimed himself King of Denmark, Norway and England.

After the death of Canute in 1035 Macbeth is reckoned to have taken the throne
of Scotland in 1040, while Edward the Confessor became King of England soon
afterwards and the building of London's Westminster Abbey started in 1052.

When Harold II became King in January 1066 it was the Norwegians who
invaded, but after his forces were weakened in successfully defending the English
from that attack, Duke William of Normandy then invaded at Hastings near the end
of the year.

How many of the other verbs in the text can you change to passive forms?

G21 Phrasal Verbs in the Passive

Can you remember the past participles for these verbs?

bring	come	blow	hang	break	take
	put	cut	run	give	set

Try to fill in the missing word in these sentences.

She is crying because her cat was _____ over last night.

We don't have any leaflets left – they have all been _____ out.

The chimney was _____ up last week in a controlled explosion.

My friend's company has been _____ over by a millionaire.

Re-write these sentences with the same meaning using a passive form.

The police took a suspect away for questioning.

A financial scandal has brought down the President's government.

They will set up the new computer system next week.

Our representative is bringing that matter up in a meeting today.

We put out thousands of recycling boxes in London every day.

Now choose which of the following verbs can be used in passive sentences. Then try to write sentences using your own ideas.

take off	get up	make up	hang up	break off
	take in	cut off	join in	run out

Section R | Reading

Reading Skills, R1-R3

The key to a successful reading activity with your students is to pitch the right questions for the text, which depends on the level of your students and what you want the students to get out of the exercise. With more difficult texts it is very important for you to be clear about an appropriate objective for your students so you can direct their activity towards this learning focus.

R1 concentrates on understanding instructions in a fun way, and is designed for use with a 5x5 grid which you could photocopy or simply draw on the board for your students to copy. The same idea could also be adapted in numerous ways.

1	2	3	4	5
6	7	8	9	10
11	12	13	14	15
16	17	18	19	20
21	22	23	24	25

Note that this worksheet also enables you to check that students can write instructions correctly themselves. An additional option at this stage is to give students a grid with 12 squares for them to write instructions using as many different verbs as possible: when they have finished, choose a grid, and roll dice to determine an instruction for students in the class, which they then have to perform...

R2 is designed to check students can read a timetable, and lends itself easily to a speaking or roleplay activity where students could ask each other any number of questions based on the timetables. Although the worksheet is based on fictional train lines, note that the place names are real, and the research task would therefore enable students to gain an understanding of the geography of London and its airports.

R3 is an introduction to internet searching for students who may not have used the internet in English. Note that this activity need not be carried out with a computer in class: as long as you have access to the internet yourself, you would be able to print out search information in advance to give to students. This idea could be used in many ways, as long as you know in advance what your activity will require students to 'search' for, so that you can provide the relevant printout of search results in class.

R1 | Following Instructions

Use a pencil and try to follow the instructions on your grid.

1) Write your name in square 1.
2) Go two squares to the right, and draw a house.
3) Go two more squares to the right, and draw a circle.
4) Go one square to the left, and draw a cup.
5) Go down one square, and write the number 44.
6) Go one square to the left, and write the number 20.
7) Go another square to the left, and write the number 15.
8) Go three squares to the right, and write the number 21.
9) Go down one square, and write the number 31.
10) Go two squares to the left, and write the number 1922.
11) Go two more squares to the left, and draw a car.
12) Go one square to the right, and write the number 17.
13) Go two more squares to the right, and write the number 12.
14) Go down one square, and add up the numbers in squares 9 and 14.
15) Go one square to the left, and write the number 82.
16) Go another square to the left, and write the number 16
17) Go one more square to the left, and write the number 19.
18) Go up two squares, and draw the sun.
19) Go down three squares and add up the numbers in squares 7 and 12.
20) Go one square to the right, and draw a fish.
21) Go up four squares and write down your birthday.
22) Go down one square and rub out the number you have written there.
23) Go two squares to the right and add 40 to the number in that square.
24) Go one square to the right and draw a hat on top of that number.
25) Go down two squares add up the numbers in squares 12 and 17.
26) Go down one square and add up the numbers in squares 9 and 14.
27) Go one square to the left and write the number 28.
28) Go another square to the left, and write the 'THE END'.

When you have finished, ask a partner to check your grid is correct.

Look at the verbs above and underline all the words which give instructions. Then make a similar task for your partner using a new grid with nine squares.

Reading a Timetable

London Airport Connections

London Heathrow	d	0651	every	2231	a	0741	every	2321
Dean Gardens Ealing		0702	20	2242		0732	20	2312
West Hampstead		0711	mins	2251		0723	mins	2303
Edmonton Green		0723	until	2303		0711	until	2251
Stansted International	a	0742		2322	d	0652		2232

London Gatwick	d	0746	every	2146	a	0856	every	2256
Sutton and Ewell		0756		2156		0846		2246
Kingston		0802	20	2202		0840	20	2240
Dean Gardens Ealing		0809		2209		0833		2233
South Harrow		0817	mins	2217		0825	mins	2225
East Barnet		0827		2227		0815		2215
Luton Airport	a	0841	until	2241	d	0801	until	2201

East Barnet	d	0822	every	2052	a	0917	every	2147
Edmonton Green		0836	30	2106		0903	30	2133
London City		0847	mins	2117		0852	mins	2122
Eden Park Bromley		0858	until	2128		0841	until	2111
Sutton and Ewell	a	0910		2142	d	0825		2055

Use the timetable information above to answer the following questions.

1. What time will I arrive at Stansted if I leave Heathrow at 6.51am?

2. What time is the next departure from Heathrow to Stansted?

3. What time will I arrive at Gatwick if I leave Luton at 8.01am?

4. What time is the next departure from Luton to Gatwick?

5. Where should I change if I want to go from Gatwick to Stansted?

6. How long should a journey from Heathrow to Gatwick take?

7. Where do I change if I travel from London City Airport to Heathrow?

8. What is the quickest route from Luton to Stansted?

Can you research the London area and draw a map of these stations?

R3 | Finding Information

Which reference source would you use to find the following information?

Match the items below.

A local company selling camping equipment   local newspaper

House phone number of a friend   dictionary

Times of trains from London to Leeds   Yellow Pages

Job adverts for local employment   The Phone Book

Meanings of unknown words   train timetable

*You are planning a camping trip, and need to buy some equipment.
What key words could you type into a search engine on the internet?*

| | Search

*Now find different websites with information about each of the following
items. Next to each one write down the name of a useful website.*

Backpacker tents

Waterproof clothing

Lightweight cooking equipment

Bikes

Emergency blankets

Survival food packs

Reading Texts and Articles, R4-R8

R4 Link to W8,
R7 to W9, R8 to V21

Again, depending on the level of your class, you may need to set tasks which emphasise gist or scanning as opposed to full comprehension: these texts are also an opportunity to cover the vocabulary, spellings, or grammar that you find within them.

R4 is a true story, which could be used with supplementary material about Windsor Castle or other museums in the UK. Note that the article is written in a colloquial style including expressions which mean more than the sum of their parts, such as 'what could go wrong?'; students could discuss formal and informal aspects of the text, or even act out the metal detector scene as a creative means for you to carry out a concept check!

R5 is a comprehension and linking words review: students construct full sentences from the text provided, which could be cut into strips for them to move around on their tables. Again, the a and b worksheets allow for differentiation within the class.

R6 works as a differentiated worksheet, or alternatively as a two-stage activity: R6a could be used for a dictation or as a listening task in which you write the sports on the board and students match them with the texts you read. R6b could then be used as a follow-up, or it could be used as a gapfill dictation instead. Note that R6a could be given to the students *after* R6b for them to check their answers and to set new follow-up tasks. Remember also that gapfill worksheets can always be adapted with clues such as the first letter of a word where appropriate.

R7 is a difficult reading text which includes descriptive language and long sentences, but the questions on the worksheet do not require the reader to understand every word in the article: picking up the main points in this way is a skill that you can demonstrate to students and thus help them gain confidence in reading authentic English, e.g. from a newspaper or the internet.

R8 is also designed to train students for reading authentic texts, with the activity requiring them to choose the correct definition of words in the article. The second half of the worksheet addresses the further skill of deducing meanings, and once again these are techniques which could be used with various texts.

R4 | Windsor Castle

This famous castle, near London, is open as a museum for the public. What do you think you can see there? Read this text to see if your ideas are mentioned. Did this teacher enjoy visiting the castle?

A student trip to Windsor Castle – what could go wrong?

My students were all adults and they had all come to England from other countries. So I was expecting them to be more familiar with the airport-style metal detector: however, some didn't want to give up the items in their pockets, while one forgot to pick his wallet up after passing through the machinery.

I brought that wallet, along with the student's jacket, with me. Then as I returned them, another student realised she had forgotten to pick up her keys after passing through the metal detector.

I went back to help her find them, but the one key that had been found, which was on a green key ring, wasn't hers. I tried to persuade her that if it wasn't there, we would have to come back later and hope it had been handed in.

Just when I had finally cajoled her into setting off, and I thought we could set foot into the castle grounds, yet another student noticed that she too had left her keys at the metal detectors.

"Was yours on a green key ring?" I asked desperately, wondering if the stress of this day would put me off teaching for life.

Fortunately that key was hers, and while I was away one of my other students found the other missing keys in the pocket of the jacket he had left with his wallet.

Finally we could get started. However, as the day went on, everything else went wrong. First of all, my students used their mobile phones inside the castle, and took photos of the jewellery, the furniture, the clothes, and the ceilings, completely disobeying both of the stipulations on the many signs. Even though that meant they were already in trouble with the security staff, then they joked about which painting they were going to come back and steal!

I was relieved to get them out of the castle but when they failed to return to the rendezvous point in time for the train I had told them we had to catch, I thought my nightmare was never going to end.

Eventually everyone got back safely and I put my feet up at home, relieved that it was all over. The classroom is much easier work every time!

What things can visitors see in the castle, according to this text?

Read the story again and try to answer these questions:

How many students left something at the metal detectors?

What items did they leave?

What do the signs say inside the castle?

What happened after this group left the castle together?

Why did the teacher think it was a nightmare that was never going to end?

R5a	Going Away for a Weekend.

Discuss with a partner the best places to go away for a weekend near where you live. Is there a place you would recommend to your teacher?

Now look at the sentences below about a weekend holiday. Did they have a good time? Put the sentences in order to make the full story.

I went to bed quite early on our first night because I was very tired from the flight.

I was really happy because I love surprises, and I had never been to Spain.

In the afternoon there were delays on the train and we were late for the dance performance we had booked.

On Saturday I had a headache and we couldn't go to the museum in the morning because it was closed.

He decided to take me for a surprise trip to Barcelona.

He was still feeling ill on the plane home and he had to spend most of the flight locked in the toilet!

It was a really boring day and then in the evening Liam ate some seafood which made him feel very ill.

We only just made it back to the airport in time.

My husband wanted to do something special to celebrate my birthday.

But I didn't sleep very well because the hotel was noisy and we didn't like it because the corridors were dirty and the rooms were too small.

On Sunday morning he was sick and he didn't want to get out of bed.

Try to make full sentences from these clauses and put the story in order.

I went to bed quite early on our first night...

I was really happy...

In the afternoon there were delays on the train...

On Saturday I had a headache ...

He decided to take me for a surprise trip to Barcelona.

He was still feeling ill on the plane home...

It was a really boring day...

On Sunday morning he was sick...

We only just made it back to the airport in time.

My husband wanted to do something special to celebrate my birthday.

But I didn't sleep very well...

...because the corridors were dirty and the rooms were too small.

...because it was closed.

...because I love surprises, ...

...and we didn't like it...

...and he had to spend most of the flight locked in the toilet!

...and we couldn't go to the museum in the morning...

...because I was very tired from the flight.

...and he didn't want to get out of bed.

...and then in the evening Liam ate some seafood...

...and I had never been to Spain.

...because the hotel was noisy...

...which made him feel very ill.

...and we were late for the dance performance we had booked.

R6a | New Sports

One of your friends wants to try out a new sport. Match the activity with the right advice...

Cycling

This is quite an expensive hobby but you can play cheaply at first if you play on a small course and hire your clubs.

Horse riding

You need to wear a helmet if it is your first time, and be careful not to try jumping over any hedges!

Skiing

Wear some gloves and a pair of trousers which will not be damaged easily. You can stay close to the edge at first – and don't worry about going fast to begin with!

Golf

This is a great way to keep fit and you can do short trips or long rides – depending how much time you have. Make sure you take lots of water.

Ice skating

This sport is very expensive and you need to take lessons if it is your first time. You also need to make sure you have the right equipment as it can be very cold.

How many sports do you know?

Think of at least five sports you have never played and write them down. Why haven't you tried these activities before?

R6b | New Sports

One of your friends wants to try out a new sport. Try to fill in the gaps in each section of advice.

Cycling

This is a great _____ to keep fit and you can do _____ trips or _____ rides – depending how much _____ you have. Make sure you take lots of water.

Horse riding

You need to _____ a helmet if it is your _____ time, and be _____ not to try jumping over _____ hedges!

Skiing

This sport is _____ expensive and you need to take _____ if it is your first time. You also need to make _____ you have the right _____ as it can be very cold.

Golf

This is quite _____ expensive hobby but you _____ play cheaply at _____ if you play on a small _____ and hire your clubs.

Ice skating

Wear some _____ and a pair of _____ which will not be _____ easily. You can stay close to the edge at first – and don't worry about going fast to _____ with!

Have you tried any of these sports before? Discuss them with a partner. Now write some advice for a friend who is thinking of trying a new keep-fit activity. Choose any sport you know, or use one of the following if you prefer: swimming, running, walking, tennis...

R7 | Stop the Bus!

This text is from the diary of a teacher on holiday in the country where he was working. Why do you think the travellers in the story might want to stop their bus? Read the article to see if one of your ideas is correct.

"Stop the bus!"

Whatever the local language, it is possible to cry out with enough urgency for anyone to understand. Our driver was already pulling over by the side of the road wondering what the problem was before the guide could translate.

Sometimes you can't wait for a bus ride to end: every traveller can remember an arduous journey – over a difficult mountain pass, across a dusty plain, or simply through endless countryside.

But closing your eyes can hide away an unexpected moment of beauty; who can know when a glimpse of the light may be enough to transform the earthly view into a heavenly one?

"Stop the bus!" We couldn't simply drive past without taking pictures here. The sudden view of the sparkling river, set on the canvas of clear blue skies fresh with the mountain air, was about to flash past our windows too quickly.

Not even the villagers gave their breathtaking view a second glance, failing to appreciate the beauty in something they had known all their lives. It was the same for the steep narrow rapids we had seen earlier on our way up through the foothills, pure white water catching the ruby morning light.

There are too many wonderful places in the world which cannot all be mapped as tourist attractions, but these are the sights that it is good to stare at – to print them permanently upon our memories.

And there are scenic gems within every country. Not everyone can go on holidays abroad, but no matter where each person lives, we can all appreciate the beauty of the natural world everywhere around us, and in our minds travel even as far away as the stars.

Do you think this journey could have taken place in the country where you live? Why, or why not?

Read the story again and try to answer these questions:

How did the driver know the passengers wanted to stop?

Where is the bus when the passengers see the river? Where are the rapids and what do the local people think about them? Why?

Why does the writer think everyone can enjoy the beauty of the world even if they can't travel to another country?

When you have finished, discuss these questions with a partner.

Have you been abroad? Where would you like to visit, and why?

Do you agree with the writer's opinions in the last two paragraphs?

Read this text and underline any words you don't know.

Shares on the stock market plunged almost ten percent yesterday. After trading had been suspended for four hours the exchange was re-opened, with the market later recovering by about five percent thanks to central bank support.

After you have read the whole paragraph, can you work out the meaning of any of the words you have underlined? Look them up in a dictionary.

Now choose the correct meaning of these words as used in this text.

a) plunge:
\# a sudden drop, dive or fall
\# to drop, dive or fall into water
\# to suddenly reduce in value

b) exchange:
\# giving or receiving something in return for something else
\# a place where shares in companies are bought and sold
\# a visit by a group of students or teachers to another country

c) suspend:
\# to officially stop or delay something for a short time
\# to hang something in the air, for example by attaching it to the ceiling
\# to send someone away from his or her school for a period of time

Now read this text and underline any words you don't know.

The company's shares have fallen by four percent due to a surge in the price of oil to record levels. Last week the airline imposed a surcharge on tickets to compensate internally for these costs.

Can you guess or work out the meaning of the following words before you find them in a dictionary? Which have 'positive' or 'negative' meanings?

compensate   surge   impose   surcharge

Reading Short Stories, R9-R13

The beauty of using short stories in English teaching is that readers want to get to the end of the story, and therefore need to read on without looking up every word along the way. They will consolidate learning by seeing words and grammar in an authentic context, and are still able to look words up afterwards.

Depending on the level of your students, however, you will need to choose which vocabulary may need to be pre-taught – possibly in advance, with a further review on the day of reading the text.

These worksheets start with a warm-up for discussion in groups, and questions are suggested for the stories on the basis that each section will be read in turn, with the reading texts photocopied (or folded) so that students cannot read ahead. Note that the question sheets do not need to be handed out to students if you would prefer to ask them verbally (or use an OHP). The stories and worksheets also introduce further discussion topics, reflecting different aspects of life in modern Britain.

As authentic texts, these stories are also used as the basis for punctuation and writing review in worksheets W11 and W17 (where the extent of new vocabulary may be more manageable).

An additional theme for readers is that each story links five items which were the specified pictures in the 2006 5photostory.com competition: a key, a park bench, an emergency exit, a petrol station and a ladder. The published anthology of the best entries, 39 Emergency Exits, contains a wonderful amount of variety for readers (and it does also include a short story of my own...)!

Meanwhile I would like to express my gratitude to authors Jaimina Bodalia, Cheryl Campbell, Daniel Goodwin, Jane Grimshaw, and Carolyn Kiff, for permission to publish the stories included here for users of No Limits – Unlimited.

Although these stories may be photocopied for use in class in accordance with the use of this book, copyright for each story remains with the author and these texts must not be reproduced in any other form without the prior consent of the author, which may be requested through contacting the publisher.

R9 English Breakfast

What food do people usually eat for breakfast in the UK?

What is known as a Full English Breakfast?

What is a B & B?

Where are the most expensive hotels in the UK?

Read the first section of this story and try to find out what time of day it is.

Where are the two people in this story?

What has happened while they were eating?

What do you think is going to happen next?

Where do the police take the people from the service station?

How long do you think they will have to wait? Why does Tommy's wife complain?

Who do you think Quentin is? Why will he be upset?

How long does Tommy go away for?

Do you think he has found the children? What do you think will happen?

What did Tommy do to help find the grandchildren?

Why do you think the boys didn't realise their grandparents were worried?

Do you think Tommy and his wife are given a fair reward for their help?

R10   Your E-mail or Your Wife?

Do you know anyone who works from home?

What do you think are the advantages and disadvantages of having your office in your house?

What are the disadvantages of spending too much time at work?

Read the start of this story and decide if Stuart is happy: is he enjoying his job?

Why does Stuart spend so much time in the garden?

How does Jenn feel about his work?

What do you think she is going to do in the next part of the story?

Was Stuart too scared to climb up the ladder into the bathroom?

Do you think he slept well that night? Why or why not?

What do you think he is going to do to make things better?

Where are the children when Stuart takes Jenn out in the car?

Why is the park a special place for him to take her?

Do you think they are going to live happily ever after?

How did Stuart and Jenn become friends when they met for the first time?

What does the expression, 'Your money or your life' mean?

Do you think Stuart has learned a lesson? Why or why not?

The View From My Kitchen Window

What kind of view do you have from your house?

How often do you look out of your windows? What can you see happening sometimes?

What kind of people would think the view from their windows is important?

Read the start of this story: how much time does this lady spend looking out of her window?

Why does the woman say the kitchen window is the best feature of her house?

What can she see outside?

What do you think is going to happen in the story?

Do you agree that a window cleaner has the best view of all? Why or why not?

What things has the woman seen happening outside her window before?

Why did she have to speak to the police?

She says that today she sees something that will change her life: what do you think it is?

What happened to her washing up when the man went in to rob the petrol station?

Did it feel to her as if the robber took a long time? Why do you think so?

What do you think her husband is going to do now he has come home?

Why isn't she going to call the police?

Why did he get the bottle of champagne and some red paint?

Why do you think they are going to move house?

Another Brian

What things would you change if you had chance to go back to another time in your life?

What do you think about the idea of travelling in time?

Why do we think about the important things in life when someone dies?

Read the start of this story and decide if you think Brian is from a close family or not.

Why is Brian sad on his birthday?

What does he see in the birthday cake?

What do you think he is going to find?

What do you think the key is for?

Why do you think the key says he should *Trust no one*?

Who do you think the attacker is? Why do you think he has kidnapped him?

Why does Brian's attacker want to take the key?

What do you think his father would do with the key?

What would you say to the other man if you were Brian?

Do you think Brian did the right thing? Why do you think the key was so important?

This is the end of the story, but what do you think Brian would do next?

In real life, we cannot change the past; how does this mean we should live every day?

R13 | The Emerald

What are the advantages and disadvantages of being a celebrity?

Who are the most famous celebrities you know? What are the characteristics of their lives?

In what ways do people treat celebrities as 'more than human'?

Read the start of this story and decide what kind of celebrities the two famous people are.

When is this story set? What year do you think it is?

What is special about the star above the building?

Who do you think they are going to meet in this restaurant?

What is the most unusual thing about the clothes Jeremy is wearing?

What is the difference between the first impressions Eleanor's parents form of Jeremy?

What do you think the staff of this impeccable restaurant will do?

In what ways are Simon and Melanie impressed with the celebrity couple?

Where have Jeremy and Eleanor been earlier in the evening?

What do you think Jeremy is going to say to Mr and Mrs Lipton?

Do you think Jeremy will survive the evening without upsetting Eleanor? Why or why not?

Does fame ensure that celebrities are people whose character others will be impressed by?

In what ways do celebrities and ordinary people all face the same realities of life?

English Breakfast

by Cheryl Campbell, Luton, UK

Hungry, we decided to stop at the next motorway service station.

"How about just one night?" I pleaded.

"Those stupid brochures!" Tommy complained, only half-jokingly. "How is it that you always sniff out the expensive places to stay?! You know we simply can't afford to go staying in those country house hotels!"

I knew the most I could look forward to being treated with was an all-day breakfast. Twenty-six years ago, that was the first thing we had found we had in common – love for a full English breakfast – and we entered the cafeteria with our mouths watering.

"*How* much?" Tommy demanded at the till. But he was right, it was a rip-off. And not even fresh. With trays in hand we searched for a window seat.

Suddenly: the exploding whoosh was visible immediately from our plastic table. The room fell into an eerie silence as everyone stared incredulously at the petrol station. Orange balls of flames leapt high.

English Breakfast by Cheryl Campbell

People were running inside towards us for safety before we heard the emergency services on their way. Two-tones and sirens blared, as emergency vehicles arrived on the scene.

Police and ambulancemen simultaneously calmed, consoled, and provided first aid, while the seriously injured were rushed to hospital, and the rest of us were ushered through an emergency exit and evacuated into a field away from the service station building.

The terrible smell of burning fuel still lingered and the police kept us moving, away from the fiery flames. They led us through a wood to a park on the edge of a small town, trying to answer everyone's questions at once.

I made a beeline for the rotting park bench in the corner of the park and slumped into it. "What about our food?" I complained. "And we're never going to get to our B&B now!"

"Don't worry, we'll get there!" said Tommy patiently. "It'll just be later than we planned, that's all. It's a chance to think of others who are needier than yourself…"

A couple of minutes later, I noticed an elderly couple come out of the woods led by a young policewoman. I immediately jumped up to offer them my place and gestured for them to come over.

"Thank you, dear," the lady said, sobbing, and as she sat on the bench she put her head in her hands. Her companion looked pale and worried as he tried to console her.

"Can I leave them with you for a minute?" the policewoman asked, as her radio crackled and she strode back off into the crowd.

I nodded as the old man spoke despairingly, apparently talking to no one except himself. "Quentin will never forgive us for this…! What is he going to say?!"

I squatted down in front of them. "Can I help?" I asked gently.

Taking her hands away from her face the lady said, "We have lost them!"

"Our grandchildren," her husband explained. "We let them go into the shop in the service station and now we haven't seen them – since the explosion."

"I'm sure they'll be all right..." I tailed off, hoping they would be. I looked up at Tommy and immediately felt happy and grateful that he was there safe with me. He winked in reply: there were times when speech wasn't necessary, we just understood each other.

"Can you tell us what they look like, what they were wearing?" he asked. "Anything that could identify them?"

The lady slowly raised her head, a sudden thought shining in her face like a ray of hope.

"Yes! Yes!" she said. "They bought those caps, in blue, with 'London' on it, they were both wearing them. You know, *caps!*"

"Baseball caps?" asked Tommy.

The lady nodded her silent reply.

"Right, let me see what I can do. You stay with them," he said to me, setting off towards the cluster of policemen keeping order at the park entrance, "and I'll meet you back here."

It seemed like he was away for an age. I sat on the bench with them and talked to the old lady to take her mind off things: anything I could think of – my part-time job, our trip to see my sister, my dreams of staying in a French chateau, the tennis on TV at the moment, how I like my eggs done...

Eventually Tommy came back.

"How did you get on?" I asked excitedly.

"That policewoman's radio wasn't working properly, for some reason," he said, shaking his head. "No one had been able to hear the message she put out before. So I've made sure they know where we are, anyway."

I was the one who saw them first. I caught a glimpse of a blue baseball cap emerging from a police car. An officer pointed to our corner of the park and then there were two tall and excited boys running towards us.

"Grandpa! Grandma!" they approached, oblivious to the pain their grandparents had been through.

"We had a ride in a police car!" one of the grandsons said excitedly.

"So you did!" said grandpa, as the two youngsters bent down into the tight cuddle he gave them.

We began quietly walking away, to leave them to it, but we hadn't gone far before the gentleman called out, "Young Man!"

We each looked over our shoulders instinctively, as he beckoned towards us.

The gentleman handed Tommy a key. There was as much puzzlement upon his face as there was on mine.

"An open invitation – to treat your good lady how she deserves to be treated," was all he said.

I was handed a 'calling card'. But this was no ordinary calling card: I immediately saw that it had an official crest.

"Take it!" he said, in a powerful voice. "Take it. Borrow the key as our way of saying thank you. Just call ahead and stay for as long as you want to. And our cook will give you the best bacon and eggs you have ever tasted!"

We had just been given the key to the Marquis of Bath's Stately Home.

The View From My Kitchen Window

by Carolyn Kiff, Milton Keynes, UK

The view from my kitchen window is great. We live in a 1930's terraced house, which goes back a long way and has big rooms. It's a real childhood house, full of corners and cupboards. But for me, our kitchen window is the best feature – or rather, the view outside.

It's not a view onto the back garden and we don't have a front garden. It's a view which keeps me in touch with the world as I wash up. My view is the hustle and bustle of the street outside my front door. I love it.

I hear one neighbour opening her front door and the bump and crash as she struggles to get her three-wheeled buggy out. We smile at each other as she passes. She raises her eyebrows and gestures, 'Should have bought a smaller one!' Her baby, Daniel, cottons on and waves just as he is going out of sight.

My other neighbour is an elderly blind man. I hear the gentle tapping of his stick mapping out the door and step for him. I knock on the kitchen window; he turns, smiles and waves. Funny how a blind person can more observant than someone with twenty-twenty vision.

Directly opposite our terraced row is a convenience store, selling the usual: loaves, light bulbs and lottery tickets. To the right of the 'Twenty-4-Seven' is a BP Petrol Station. To the left is another terraced row, regimented and saluting at me. There is a gap between two of the homes, and through this narrow passageway is the local park. I often take a stroll that way and eat a Twix on the park bench, watching the children swing higher and higher.

The View From My Kitchen Window by Carolyn Kiff

If it wasn't for washing up I would still be ignorant of cars, but I can tell you all sorts now – makes and models, hatchbacks and saloons, convertibles and 4 x 4's. The petrol station sees it all and so do I. 'Yes,' I think to myself, 'my kitchen window has the best view!'

Just as I'm wringing out my dishcloth I hear a familiar clatter of the window cleaner's ladder being propped up against the house. Looking up I smile and nod at him, 'No, he has the best view…into all those houses!' I think to myself.

I've seen some crises unfolding before my window. My elderly neighbour was nearly mown down by a car screeching off the petrol forecourt. Somebody stole petrol. Silly really – don't people know all petrol stations have signs saying, "All drive offs are reported to the police," and cameras recording the licence plates? I witnessed it all and hastened into the street to save my neighbour with my yellow marigolds still adorning my hands! He was OK, a little shaken; the ambulance took him to hospital for observation. It turned out the police needed my statement; the cameras are just for show – no film.

But that was another day; the scene I witnessed today would change my life.

The window cleaner had come and gone. I took my gloves off and sent a quick text to my husband. I thought I'd finished the washing up but when I checked the kitchen I'd forgotten the pots and pans I had been cooking dinner with. They were still on the stove, food-splattered and grimy. I sighed and wished for the hundredth time I had space for a dishwasher. I dutifully refilled the bowl and gave another squirt of liquid and watched the bubbles form and multiply. Donning my gloves, I got on with my job – washing up and keeping up with the people-watching outside.

The View From My Kitchen Window by Carolyn Kiff

The garage was quiet mid-afternoons, with very few cars coming to refuel. I took note of every car that graced the station that afternoon; a sapphire blue Focus caught my eye. The forecourt was completely empty so the driver was able to park in a parking space near the shop. He got out, and I watched open-mouthed, watering trickling over the rim of my bowl, as he rammed a dark balaclava onto his head and marched into the shop, holding a pistol. I didn't hear exactly what was being said but I discerned shouting and banging and witnessed the raider angrily gesturing to get his money. This seemed to be happening in slow motion. Actually, it took 35 seconds for him to storm in, point a gun, grab the cash and, oddly, a bottle of champagne, storm out, jump back into the Focus, insert the key, and speed off. The BP staff gathered their senses quickly and came running out of all doors, the side emergency exit banging as it was flung wide, but the Focus was quickly out of sight leaving the bewildered staff pacing the forecourt and using mobiles to call the police.

My mouth shut and I swallowed with difficulty, it was so dry. I took a deep breath and held onto the edge of the sink to steady myself and collect my thoughts, which seemed to swim before my eyes.

My heart thumping away, I was still frozen to the sink when I heard a car pull into our garage. The back door opened. "Honey, I'm back!" came a familiar voice with a familiar greeting.

The View From My Kitchen Window by Carolyn Kiff

I suppressed my thumping chest, put on a new countenance and smiled. "Sweetheart! You're back! How did you get on today – first day on a new job? You'll never guess what I've just seen; I think perhaps I should call the police…"

"Now sweetie, why would you do that? – I brought you a present as well." A bottle of champagne ceremoniously plonks onto the dinning table as arms envelop me in a bear hug of love.

"How did you get on? Anyone see me?" came a whisper down my neck. "I've locked the Focus in the garage," he continued gently. "I've already got the spray paint. Red. Thought we'd be a bit different, I've gone off blue for a Focus!"

I giggled as the reassuring arms calmed my beating heart till I felt it no more. "Nope, nobody saw you, just me… my kitchen window really does have the best view; pity we have to leave it behind when we move again. All lookout posts should be like my kitchen window."

Your E-mail or Your Wife?

by Jane Grimshaw, Warrington, UK

Stuart looked down at the shiny new key in his hand. It was the key to his own space; somewhere he could have peace and quiet to do his work. He turned the key in the keyhole and then admired his brand new office, in the form of a shed.

It wasn't long before Stuart was nicely settled into his new domain. Everything had its place and there were no noisy distractions from the house any more; in fact, he felt that he was beginning to enjoy it too much. He thumbed through some papers and then headed off in the direction of the house.

"Oh, Stuart, nice to see you! I sometimes wonder if you realise that you have two children and a wife," said Jenn sarcastically.

"Oh, sorry love," replied Stuart, kissing her on the cheek. "I've just popped in to check my email."

Jenn muttered quietly to herself and then continued with the tea. She hardly saw Stuart these days. He didn't spend much time with the twins any more either. When he said an office in the garden would be less distracting, she never imagined how much time he would spend out there. He went out first thing in the morning and stayed out there all day and evening, only popping in and out of the house briefly to check his email. He occasionally even ate out there.

Jenn was really beginning to feel neglected. If it wasn't for that stupid computer being in the house, then she would probably never see him at all.

Once the twins were in bed, Jenn went into the kitchen to make herself a drink. She looked down the garden – he was still in there. She screwed up her face angrily and decided it was time she taught Stuart a lesson.

Your E-mail or Your Wife? by Jane Grimshaw

Stuart popped into the house later on to do his usual, last email check of the day. Jenn waited until he had returned to his office and then she locked the back door, turned off the lights and went to bed.

It was well after midnight when Stuart realised how late it was. He finished off what he was doing and then came out and locked the shed.

He walked over to the back door and pushed the handle down, and then again. It suddenly occurred to him that there were no lights on and then it dawned on him.

"Oh no! What does she think she's playing at?"

Stuart moaned and cursed, as he tried to think of an answer to his dilemma and then he noticed the small window in the bathroom was open.

"Ladders!" he said. "Phew, what a good job I never got round to padlocking them."

He cringed as he put the ladders up to the window – he hated heights. He climbed carefully up and then tried to pull himself through the opening, but it was no use, he was too big; only a child would be able to get through there. So, tired and fed up, he climbed back down the ladders and prepared for a night in the garden – at least it was summer and not the middle of winter.

It was a long night and as Stuart eventually calmed down he began to think about why Jenn was so hurt and angry with him. He started to realise that he hadn't paid her any attention for ages, or Ellie and Alex. He would make it up to them. Work would not be his top priority any more.

When Jenn arrived home from work on Thursday, Stuart was waiting for her with a cup of tea.

"As it is your day off tomorrow, we are going to have a day out, just the two of us, and mum and dad are going to collect the twins from school and keep them for the night. Then, on Saturday we are all going to spend a nice family day together."

Jenn was speechless; she wished that she had locked him out sooner.

Friday was a beautiful day. Stuart climbed into the driver's seat of Jenn's car and they set off up the road in high spirits, but it wasn't long before Stuart glanced at the fuel gauge.

"Oh no, Jenn, why didn't I remember how bad you are at filling your car up with petrol!"

"It'll be fine, I always run it on empty. You worry too much," replied Jenn.

Stuart wasn't going to take any chances, so he pulled into the nearest petrol station, but he was determined that nothing was going to spoil the day.

Finally, they arrived at some park gates and Stuart waited for some reaction from Jenn.

"Roxford Park! We haven't been here for ages. I wonder if our bench is still standing," exclaimed Jenn, and she rushed out of the car.

"I'm so glad it's still here," she said, running her fingers over the etched heart that contained their names.

Stuart sat next to her and put his arm round her.

"Yeah, they were good times weren't they," he said. "It just seems so long ago now."

The restaurant was the perfect end to the day: soft music, wine and candlelight. Jenn felt like she had taken a step back in time with Stuart and hadn't enjoyed herself so much in ages.

She looked around the room and suddenly started to laugh. "I've just spotted that Emergency Exit and it brings back memories of when we first met at Julie and Jeff's wedding. I can still see the expression on your face now."

"How could I forget that, I've probably still got the bruises," replied Stuart.

"Just think if the fire bell hadn't gone off and we hadn't struggled with that stupid Emergency Exit door, then we might never have met."

It was late when they arrived home. Jenn giggled like a schoolgirl in the hall and pulled Stuart upstairs with her. She turned to face him – it was wonderful to have him back at last; she had really missed him.

All of a sudden, Stuart shot out of her grasp and rushed out of the bedroom.

"What's wrong?" demanded Jenn. "Where are you going?"

"Oh, can't you just wait a minute... I just need to check my email – I haven't checked it all day!"

Another Brian

by Daniel Goodwin, Hackney, London

Brian stared down solemnly at the half-eaten birthday cake and sighed. It was the last thing Mother had made before her death. He wondered if she took more pleasure in making the cake than he did in eating it.

Picking up the kitchen knife from the table, Brian cut out a large triangle and shovelled it sloppily into his mouth as a child would devour it. Thirty-four years of age and here he was sitting alone at a kitchen table wailing like an upset infant. It was less than a week since the heart attack struck but the impact of her death still weighed Brian down.

As the sponge went moist in his mouth Brian spotted a strange object buried within the depth of the cake before him. It was a small burgundy box, the type that would contain a ring or a set of cufflinks.

Brian picked up the knife, stabbed at the sponge surrounding the buried box and then pulled it out. He brushed the crumbs away from the surface and without hesitation opened it up.

At first Brian expected mum to have hidden an old long-lost family heirloom in the cake as a surprise present. The priceless ring of a great-grandfather or a pair of gold cufflinks she had found gathering dust in the cellar, but no. Even more shocked was Brian by the fact that it was nothing he expected.

Another Brian by Daniel Goodwin

All that sat in the box was a small, shiny, silver key.

It looked like the type that would open a filing cabinet or a safety deposit box. Brian swallowed his mouthful and picked the key up out of its box and on closer inspection noticed two words inscribed on its base. *Trust no one*.

Brian figured the best person to query about this was his father and decided to pay him an immediate visit.

Dad's house was only ten minutes' drive… but he had to turn into a petrol station to top up the car.

As he entered the shop Brian noticed a sweaty looking man in a dirty coat follow him into the store, suspiciously pacing the aisles with his head bowed.

Brian was about to pay for his petrol when the man grabbed his arm, twisted it behind his back and forced him through the emergency exit.

Before Brian could speak he was hurled through the open back doors of a transit van parked at the back of the petrol station.

The guy climbed in the van after Brian and slammed the huge metal doors behind them on entering. He was about twenty years older than Brian but there was a slight resemblance which made Brian briefly wonder if this assailant was related.

But then he yelped as the attacker pinned him face down to the floor, locked his hands behind his back and applied handcuffs.

"What is this?" Brian stammered in shock

"I know everything about the key."

"What do you mean?"

"I need to stop you. To change the future. You were on your way to your father's."

"Yeah."

"To ask him about the key..."

"Yes."

"You mustn't give him that key."

"Why?"

"I dare not say."

"Well what if I say no?"

The man took out a gun from his inside pocket and aimed at his own head. "Then my life, and eventually your life, will not be worth living."

"You threaten me with your life? You're insane!"

"Give me the key Brian!"

Out of panic and sheer terror Brian kicked the man square in the face and was able to leap through the back doors of the van and out into the night.

He ran confused into the forest without looking back.

Brian continued for about five minutes before noticing a rotting park bench directly in front of him, an old ladder to the left and then just beyond that, a steep drop into a stream that stretched off into the distance in both directions.

Brian panicked as he suddenly realised he was trapped: he could hear the footsteps of his pursuer approaching.

He collapsed frustrated and breathless onto the park bench as the other man emerged from within the woods and raised the gun.

"I need that key," he shouted.

"No! Why should I believe you?"

"Trust me Brian. I *am* you, from the future."

Brian paused in shock. "If that's true... then if you kill me *you* will die."

"Better to be dead than face the consequences of leaving here empty-handed."

"What happens in the future?" asked Brian, incredulous.

"You can never know. If I tell you, the circumstances will unfold as they did in my timeline and nothing will change."

Brian stared down at the ground and remembered the words his mother had engraved into the key. *Trust no one.* He thought for a long time before he realised what he must do.

"OK," he said decisively. "But first you'll have to take my handcuffs off."

The older man put his gun down with relief and bent over Brian's wrists to unlock him. As soon as he had undone one of the locks, Brian lashed out, catching the man in the eye, and making him drop the key. With his attacker briefly off-balance, Brian lifted him up and threw him into the ravine.

He quickly picked up the key and thought about taking the gun, but then kicked it into the stream before running straight back to his car.

Should he still go to his dad's house? *Trust no one.* It was only when he pulled his mother's key out of his pocket that he realised what it opened. His mother's key unlocked the remaining handcuff which was still flailing on his wrist.

The Emerald

by Jaimina Bodalia, Harrow, London

The Emerald restaurant towered dramatically against the inky sky. The October landscape gave the impression of a delicate canvas; a backdrop for the elaborate 1930's architecture of modern London's finest dining haunt. Golden exterior lighting adorned the building, accentuating its splendour.

A single solitary star shimmered in its place, centre stage above the restaurant. Upon seeing a young couple approaching the back entrance, it dimmed for a moment as if winking, before resuming its scintillating act.

The other stars lay hidden in the wings, delaying their arrival for fear of upstaging the undeniably gorgeous couple.

Other mere mortals such as the two girls en route to their bus stop felt privileged even to cross this celebrity couple's path: one of the young women gasped an "O" of surprise, while the other stared unashamedly. Unfortunately, before either could coax their tongue from the roof of their mouth and conjure up the desired words to express their delight; the couple were gone.

All that lay in their wake was one final, sharp click of designer heels on the pavement and a distinctive masculine scent lingering in the air, as the girls had to catch their breath on a nearby park bench.

A door attendant, dressed in a designer suit and fedora, opened the restaurant's emergency exit, which was being disguised as a secret entrance for the elite.

The restaurant lobby was paved in marble and lit with crystal chandeliers. Once inside, a charming maitre d' instantly materialised at their side. He greeted them warmly and guided them towards a set of heavy red velvet curtains. After emerging through these in what one can only describe as a theatrical fashion, the couple found themselves in the main dining area.

She glanced around this room full of the world of showbiz with a nonplussed expression on her face as she led the way to a table in the corner.

The Emerald by Jaimina Bodalia

"Mum, dad... this is Jeremy," Eleanor Lipton gestured proudly to the gentleman (and I use the term gentleman in the loosest way possible) standing beside her: although they were dining in a high-class restaurant, a favourite amongst many celebrities such as Gwyneth Paltrow and the Material Girl herself, Madonna, it was indisputable that Eleanor's guest looked rather out of place. While Eleanor was the picture of perfection in a pale pink chiffon dress with pink diamonds to match, her date, on the other hand, seemed to prefer the understated look.

Sporting tattered black jeans, a shabby dinner jacket (which upon closer inspection was merrily decorated with food stains) and three days' worth of stubble, it was safe to say that The Emerald restaurant had *never,* in all its years, seen a character such as Jeremy Francis descend its immaculate steps before.

After Eleanor's quick introduction, our man in question reached across the table and shook Mr Lipton's hand, while barely making eye contact. A small gold earring in the shape of a key hung dangerously low from his left earlobe.

Mrs Lipton, on the other hand, received a rather slow and intense once-over with his dark eyes. This was followed by a small, knowing smile. The poor lady, who had not been gazed at with such fervour or avid interest in many years now, (much less by a younger man!) blushed furiously like a schoolgirl.

Fortunately, the moment went unnoticed by Mr Lipton, who was still staring shamelessly at the young man's attire with his mouth slightly open.

No Limits – Unlimited

Jeremy pulled out Eleanor's chair and she gracefully seated herself. He then pulled out his own and dropped heavily into it, his expression unreadable. A waiter immediately appeared at their side.

It was Simon's first day and he had already managed to offend two tables by mixing up their orders, not to mention a slight mishap concerning a middle-aged actress in a dress two sizes too small for her and a bottle of red wine. He had been having a miserable night – until now, that is, when he found himself staring for real into those sensual eyes, completely mesmerised by their long, dark lashes.

Meanwhile his colleague Melanie arrived with a genius plan that granted her an acceptable reason to pay the table a visit: she presented the four of them with complimentary drinks on the house, praising Jeremy for what she had already heard from other diners to have been a fine stage debut. Jeremy returned the compliment with a lopsided grin and Melanie forgot to breathe.

"Sorry we're late," said Eleanor, dismissing these servers with her eyes, "but we couldn't shake everyone off after they were congratulating us on the show tonight. We also made a quick stop at the petrol station on the way. Then of course, once we got here we couldn't find a safe place to park Jeremy's motorbike."

Mrs Lipton gasped. "Motorbike?" she whispered.

"Is something wrong, mother?" Eleanor asked.

"You rode here on a motorbike? In *that* dress?" Mrs Lipton was careful to keep her voice down for fear that any of the other diners might happen to overhear their conversation and make the *terrible* mistake of believing that her daughter made a *habit* of travelling on motorbikes. Not that they could have heard, mind you.

It pained Jeremy to know that the mindless chatter all around him was drowning out the harmonies of the soft jazz music playing in the background.

"Oh yes! It is the fastest and most enjoyable way to travel. I *highly* recommend it," replied Eleanor.

"Hmm… yes… well, I think I would rather stick to the Rolls, thank you dear," Mrs Lipton answered, by now rather agitated. Her discomfort, however, seemed to go unnoticed by her daughter, who casually turned to her father and beamed her brightest smile.

"Dad, how are you?"

By this time, Mr Lipton had managed to pull himself out of his initial state of shock and tear his eyes away from the young hoodlum that was courting his only daughter.

"Oh, I'm all right, sweet pea," he answered faintly. He then paused a moment before slowly glancing at Jeremy. "And, how are you, then?" he asked hesitantly.

At this point in time, Jeremy had still not spoken. He had yet to comment on Mr Lipton's toupee, which he had found *impossible* not to notice from the first moment Eleanor had singled out her parents. After close inspection, he discovered that he was able to count the number of strips of tape required to fix it firmly into place.

Jeremy had also failed to mention how Mrs Lipton bore a striking resemblance to that old woman off the telly. Well, minus the friendly smile, anyway. Oh, and the purple hair, of course.

Glancing up at Mr Lipton, Jeremy merely shrugged. Perhaps silence was a wise move, he pondered. Because if he opened his mouth, it would surely put a drastic end to the dinner and Eleanor had made it perfectly clear that if they got through the entire evening without incident, she would make it worth his while.

Section S | Speaking and Discussion

Introductory Dialogues, S1-S3

Speaking activities are often the hardest to co-ordinate and monitor, but once students understand the rationale behind the activity they are an essential part of your class.

Students may not at first see the point of a paired speaking activity when you clearly cannot monitor every conversation. Not only can students help correct each other, however, but the rehearsal of new grammar, tenses, vocabulary, or any other English, is a key aspect of getting their brain into a 'groove' which is reinforced by continual speaking exercises.

In general classes, a speaking task in pairs is also valuable as a means of giving students a chance to practise instead of being thrown in 'cold' when you want to choose someone to speak.

Feedback on mistakes is obviously very important, whether in monitoring pairs as you move around the class, or in sensitively highlighting something said by an individual, and a central part of the success of speaking activities is generating a mentality whereby each student listens to and 'owns' an answer given by anyone else in the class: even though this may sound obvious, it is something which is easily overlooked. Your students need to learn from the feedback you give to another student, and only if they apply it in their own spoken English are they truly learning.

Writing a dialogue also acts as a stepping stone to speaking, as writing provides a little extra 'thinking' time, but the aim of these activities is to use them as preparation for 'real' speaking.

S1 is centred on telephone phrases and finishes with a roleplay activity leaving a message.

S2 looks at making requests, especially 'would like' with an option to specify other grammar, and vocabulary such as 'could you' or 'would you mind', for students to use in conversation.

S3 uses and reviews functions for making suggestions.

Telephone English

Which sentences could you use to answer the telephone?

Can I speak to Mr Smith, please?

Hello, my name is Jane Jones.

Hello, Alison speaking.

How are you?   Who is this?

Good morning, IT Department.

Put these sentences in order to make a telephone conversation between two people, A and B. You must use all of the sentences except one.

Hello, John. This is Sally. How are you?
They're fine.
I'm sorry, he's out for lunch at the moment.
Can I leave a message?
I'm OK, thanks.
OK. Do you know when he will be back?
I'm fine thank you. And you?
Hello, extension 6543.
Would you like to leave a message?
Is Tony there?
I'm not sure. Maybe at 2 o'clock.
How are the children?

Try to put these words in order to make common telephone phrases.

? you back her please ask me could to call
? I him call to back shall you ask
? your he has number got
at here not moment the he's.
not afraid office in I'm today she's the.
? give to you number would her you mobile like me

Roleplay a conversation with a partner in which one of you wants to leave a message...

S2   Making Requests Dialogues

Think of some places or situations where you sometimes need to make requests. Write down some of the words you might use at these times.

Now complete the conversation using 'like' or 'would like'

Canteen Assistant: What's your favourite food?

Student: _____ .

Canteen Assistant: We haven't got that today, I'm afraid! What would you like instead?

Student:_____ .

Canteen Assistant: Anything else?

Student: Yes please. _____ .

Canteen Assistant: Would you like a drink? The milk is on special offer today!

Student:_____ .

Canteen Assistant: No problem!

Student: By the way, what do you usually like to eat for lunch?

Canteen Assistant:_____ .

Now hold a conversation with a partner with one of you making requests in a place or situation that you choose. You must use 'would like' and the other words or grammar which your teacher writes on the board.

When you have finished, write your conversation as an A-B dialogue.

S3 | Making Suggestions

Your friend is bored. Make suggestions for what they could do.

You could... Why don't you...?   I think you should...

Unfortunately your friend has no money. Make some more suggestions of what you could do together.

Let's...   Shall we...   ?   Why don't we...?

Do you find it difficult to think of ideas for birthday presents? Can you correct the mistakes in this advice about buying presents?

It is more better to give a gift chocolate.

I will give on a present special occasions.

Kitchen things is good idea.

I would give diaries, are always popular.

Now work in pairs to complete this conversation with your ideas.

A: I need to buy a present for one of my friends.
B: What _____ ?
A: I don't know. I hate shopping!
B: Why _____?
A: Hmmm. That might be too expensive.
B: You could _____.
A: That's a good idea.
B: Let's _____.
A: Thanks! Are you sure you have enough time today?
B: No problem. OK, where _____?

When you have finished, work with a new partner and hold a conversation discussing your ideas about giving someone a present...

Roleplay Situations and Discussions, S4-S8   S5 Link to W22

Roleplays and discussion topics provide engaging opportunities for students to practise their speaking, and to review specific expressions which may be used in certain situations. Again the main aims are twofold: to help students train themselves in their own speaking, and to provide opportunities for you to monitor their work and sensitively correct errors.

One way of providing feedback that can work very well is to roam around the room monitoring, noting errors you will choose to highlight, and then to write them on the board or present them back to the class without revealing who made each mistake. Again it is imperative to make sure that every student realises that all of your feedback is relevant to them.

S4 concentrates on giving advice, where paired students have the same instructions: worksheets like this can be cut into strips so that students don't jump ahead to the next situation.

S5 matches up pairs with separate roles in order to generate a complaint discussion between them, and works best if it is cut up before the class so the various situations A, B, and C are distributed throughout the group, and then rotated accordingly.

S6 concentrates on discussions in which one student has to try to persuade their partner to agree to something, and these can also be cut up, if only to ensure that students spend enough time on each situation before moving on to the next one.

S7 continues with various discussion topics which rely on the students to come up with suitable opinions and ideas.

S8 presents two menus which might be found in different restaurants in the UK. Obviously there is potential for vocabulary work here, and for students to design a menu of their own traditional food and drink.

Meanwhile you may want to review the use of 'some' and 'any' before (or as a result of) your students' roleplay work, and you may find it helpful to review vocabulary for politely agreeing and disagreeing, for the various 'true or false' discussions.

S4 | Roleplays Giving Advice

You are going to think together about advice you would give someone else in different situations.

You both work in a shop.

A new member of staff is starting work today – but they have never worked in a shop before. What advice will you give them to help them when they arrive?

You both live in the same street.

A friend of yours is going to move into the same street as you, but they don't know your area very well. What advice will you give them before they move in?

You both have a friend with a very young baby.

She often gets lonely because she always has to look after her child. What advice would you give her so that she can make some more friends?

You both know someone who wants to study English.

You have a friend who is thinking about starting an English course. What advice would you give them before they enrol for a class?

| S5 | Complaints Roleplays |

| A1 | You bought a mobile phone from an electronics shop last week, but you can't re-charge the battery. You go to the shop to complain. |

| B1 | You have ordered some DVDs from an advert in the newspaper, but you had to wait six weeks and then you received the wrong films. You telephone the company to complain. |

| C1 | You decided to change internet server but now you cannot connect to the internet. You telephone the company to complain. |

| A2 | You work for an electronics shop – one of your customers comes to the shop to complain. You have to deal with their complaint. |

| B2 | You work for a DVD mail order company, and one of your customers telephones you to complain. You have to speak to them. |

| C2 | You work for an internet service provider, and one of your customers telephones you to complain. You have to deal with their complaint. |

S6 | Discussion Topics: Persuasion

You are going to work as A and B in different discussion situations.
Try to persuade your partner of your point of view.

Situation 1

A and B are very good friends. You share a flat together, but
A thinks B doesn't do enough work in the house, and wants
to persuade him/her to do more. (A starts the discussion.)

Situation 2

A and B are friends. B doesn't have a car but wants to
borrow A's car for the weekend, and has to persuade him/her
to lend it. (B starts the discussion.)

Situation 3

A is staying in a hotel, where B is the manager. A is not
satisfied with the hotel room, and finds the manager to
explain what is wrong. A wants to persuade the manager to
give him/her a new room. (A starts the discussion.)

Situation 4

A and B are neighbours. B complains about a tall tree in A's
garden and wants to persuade A to chop it down because it
is dangerous. (B starts the discussion.)

S7 | Discussion Topics

You are going to work as A and B in different situations. You will have to give or ask for information, and discuss your opinions about different topics.

A is interested in a second-hand car which is for sale. Find out about it by asking B.

B's friend has to choose between going to university or taking a well-paid job. B wants to ask for A's opinion.

A attends a conference on how to encourage children to have a healthier lifestyle, and asks B for advice and his /her opinions.

Your English teacher asks you if there are any aspects of your course you would like improved or changed. Discuss your opinions together.

B is in a shop and wants to buy a bicycle. Find out from A, the shopkeeper, which one is best.

Your teacher asks you to give some advice to other students about preparing for a speaking test. Plan what you are going to say together.

A and B have to go on TV together. You are interviewed about what you think the most important world event during the last year was. Discuss this topic.

S8 | What Would you like to Order?

Country Squire

Restaurant

Baked Salmon with sauté potatoes, and
roasted vegetables. £12.99
Grilled Dover Sole with new potatoes
and mixed vegetables. £12.99
Mussels, Scallops, & King Prawns à la
Crème, with mixed vegetables. £13.99
Battered Cod served with traditional
chips & mushy peas. £9.99
Spinach & Asparagus Pastry, with sauté
potatoes and white cheese sauce. £9.99
Beef Wellington with roasted potatoes
and roast vegetables. £12.99
Pork and Apple Bangers with creamy
mash and roasted vegetables. £12.99

Look at this menu of traditional English food. Discuss what you would order.

Roleplay with a partner: roles of customer and waiter / waitress in this restaurant.

Discuss: True or False?

Most British people eat food like this at least once a week.

Britain has many of its own traditional foods.

Now look at this takeaway menu. Discuss which countries this food is from.

Roleplay with a partner: making a telephone order.

Discuss: True of False?

Most British people eat food like this at least once a week.

British people often cook dishes which are not traditionally British food.

It's a Small World

International Takeaway Cuisine

Large Pizza, any four toppings. £6.99
Medium Pizza, any two toppings. £5.99
Lamb or Chicken Tandoori, with pilau
rice and garlic nan bread. £6.99
Lamb or Chicken Korma, Dhansak, or
Bhuna, with pilau rice and nan. £6.99
Pork or Chicken Teriyaki Rice Donburi,
with a cup of miso soup. £6.99
Quarter Shredded Duck, with pancakes,
cucumber and boiled rice. £6.99
Sweet and Sour Pork or Chicken with
egg fried rice. £6.99
Sizzling barbecued pork or beef, with a
bowl of spicy vegetable noodles. £6.99

<u>Speaking Games, S9-S11</u>

Tongue-twisters are a great way to have fun in class and it is always possible to make 'easy' tongue-twisters which are nevertheless hard for our students. Time each speaker with a stopwatch as an inducement to make them go faster!

<u>S9</u> first gives students the task of making sentences from the words provided, and although there are other possibilities which are not incorrect, my answers here are:

Fred felt fine filling files for fun.
Big bad Boris broke Bill's back before breakfast.
Stupid Sam spilt Stan's super soup on his sister Sue's shoes.
She's selling small cheap chops in the Hotshot shop.

Hotshot is the arbitrary name of a shop – chosen to make the task more fun! These sentences may be a little hard for students who are not confident speakers, but adapt them if so.

<u>S10</u> functions as a round-the-class game with each student contributing the next word in a sentence. Firstly students write down review sentences using the basic constructions in the framework boxes. In the speaking game, the group's sentence then starts off using this as a prompt (e.g. the example shown, 'I have a tap and I use it every day') and then students have to add one word each in a way that is grammatically possible: the example uses 'when' as a linking word but students have to think of their own ways to extend the sentence.

Once you have demonstrated the rules, students can then play in groups. The idea of using a grammatically simple sentence is that students need to be confident enough to add their words quickly, but the task self-differentiates to the level of language they use, and thus will still function as a review of mistakes.

<u>S11</u> works as a group game in which the teacher keeps each team's score on the board: you can award points for the number of seconds someone does speak for, if appropriate. If you prepare additional topics for more advanced students, note that you can use a topic from the worksheet as differentiation for weaker students, as they have already practised them.

Can you put the words in order to make a correct sentence?

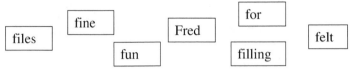

files · fine · fun · Fred · for · filling · felt

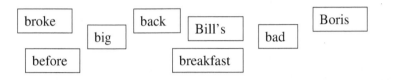

broke · big · back · Bill's · bad · Boris · before · breakfast

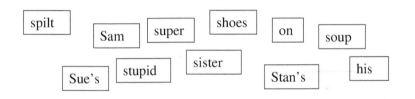

spilt · Sam · super · shoes · on · soup · Sue's · stupid · sister · Stan's · his

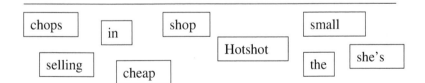

chops · in · shop · small · selling · Hotshot · cheap · the · she's

Next, practise reading the sentences out loud. Who can read each one quickest in your group?

| S10 | Household Game |

First, choose from the words below to help you write two sentences.

I have	a (an)	cupboard sink	in my house
	the	wardrobe cooker	in my flat
or		tap dishwasher	in my kitchen
	two	washing machine	in my bathroom
I use		bath radiator	in my living room
	three	shower toilet	
		bookcase shelf	every day
	four	armchair sofa	every morning
		curtains shutters	every week
		staircase ladder	
		roof TV aerial	

1) I have _____ .

2) I use _____ .

Now you are going to make sentences in pairs by speaking one word each in turn until you have made a complete sentence with this pattern:

I have _____ and I use <it/them> _____ <because/for/when>...

Each player must try to make the sentence longer, for example:

I have a tap in my kitchen and I use it every morning when I...
- wash
- up
- after
- my
- breakfast
- or
… etc

Be careful with your speaking: when you play this game in a group with your teacher you will lose a point for a grammatical mistake, or if you repeat any of the words or phrases in the boxes!

S11 | Just a Minute: Speaking Game

Can you talk about a subject for one minute?

In this game you have to work in teams to talk about subjects your teacher will give you. Some examples are given below for you to practise in pairs. (Maybe you will be given one of these topics, or maybe you will be given a different topic.)

When you start speaking you have to try to keep going for one minute. If you pause for too long, or repeat the same idea, your teacher will stop the clock and pass the topic to the next team. Your team cannot help you when you are speaking.

If someone from another group fails to complete a minute of talking, the topic might be handed to you. You cannot repeat the ideas that another speaker has already talked about, so listen carefully during the game! Whoever is speaking after one minute of each topic will score the points for that round. Good luck!

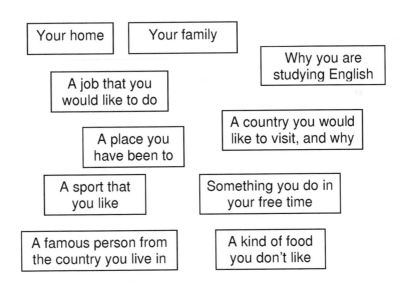

Your home

Your family

Why you are studying English

A job that you would like to do

A country you would like to visit, and why

A place you have been to

A sport that you like

Something you do in your free time

A famous person from the country you live in

A kind of food you don't like

S12 functions as a review of tenses in the context of a spoken conversation, and includes vocabulary such as 'the big 3-0' which would only normally be used in informal spoken English. This dialogue shows how a conversation can jump from one tense to another, and is intended as an incentive to help students use different tenses correctly in their own speech.

This group of S12 worksheets also provides an example of a three-way differentiation, and the same principles can be applied to any text: one way of making a worksheet more difficult is to mix up the word order of each sentence, and an additional level of difficulty is added by taking out a word of each sentence, which students then have to choose from a list.

S13 is a detailed roleplay in separate stages, where students have to contrast the informal language they would use with a friend with words they would use if talking to an official such as a policeman or a paramedic.

The worksheet also asks students to practise vocabulary they could use in a situation where they have to give sympathy to someone; meaning is also conveyed by tone of voice, of course, and this is something you may be able to model for the students to imitate in their conversations.

S14 is designed for students to read aloud, using tone of voice to emphasise the feelings of their characters: when they have finished, they can discuss who they agree with, and I like to follow this up with a roleplay task in which they have to argue the opposite case to the one they have just read out. Meanwhile S14b offers some further ways to focus on conversational skills as an optional preliminary to S14c.

S15 uses intermediate level discussion topics which require students to express complicated opinions.

S16 suggests topics for a presentation to the class by each of your students, and emphasises the importance of fluency and eye contact, which are also important in conversation.

The Conversation at Julie's Party

Each line has a verb missing, which you have to choose from the list at the bottom of the page, and complete the sentence with the correct tense.

Hi Tommy, how _____ you?

Fine, thanks – I _____ the party.

I can't _____ Julie's reached the big 3-0!

Nor can she! Did you _____ her face when she opened her cards?

But it's good fun when Julie's friends _____ together. It's a great party!

Yes – and I_____to some of her work friends that I didn't know.

Have you _____Kerry before?

No, but I _____ about her!

I can't wait for her to _____.

It's amazing that she_____a famous film star!

I remember when she was a girl – but she always _____ she wanted to be an actress!

arrive	get	enjoy	chat		
be	become		see		meet
say	hear		believe		

Do you think it is easy to go to an old school friend's party if you are famous? Think about what might happen to Kerry when she arrives, and roleplay her conversation in your pair or group.

S12b | The Conversation at Julie's Party

Put the words in order to make a conversation at Julie's party. Each sentence has a verb missing, which is in brackets at the end, but you have to decide what tense it should be.

Tommy, how you hi? <be>

the thanks – party fine, I.   <enjoy>

reached I the Julie's can't big 3-0!   <believe>

she nor can! face her when cards she her did you opened?

<see>

Julie's good friends but when it's together fun. great a it's party!

<get>

I that yes – friends and her some know work I to of didn't. <chat>

Kerry you before have?   <meet>

her about no I but!   <hear>

wait I can't to her for   <arrive>

famous a that star she it's film amazing!   <become>

girl – actress wanted she to remember when an she was be a I but she always!

<say>

Do you think it is easy to go to an old school friend's party if you are famous? Think about what might happen to Kerry when she arrives, and roleplay her conversation in your pair or group.

S12c | The Conversation at Julie's Party

Put the words in order to make a conversation at Julie's party. Each line has a verb missing, which you have to choose from the list at the bottom of the page, and then complete each sentence with the correct tense. Be careful because you can only use each verb once.

Tommy, how you hi?

the thanks – party fine, I.

reached I the Julie's can't big 3-0!

she nor can! face her when cards she her did you opened?

Julie's good friends but when it's together fun. great a it's party!

I that yes – friends and her some know work I to of didn't.

Kerry you before have?

her about no I but!

wait I can't to her for

famous a that star she it's film amazing!

girl – actress wanted she to remember when an she was be a I but she always!

arrive	get	enjoy	chat	be
become	see	meet		say
hear		believe		

Do you think it is easy to go to an old school friend's party if you are famous? Think about what might happen to Kerry when she arrives, and roleplay her conversation in your pair or group.

S13 An Accident or Emergency

1. *Imagine that one of your friends has had an accident. Choose some of these words to help you write 3 sentences describing what happened.*

fell parked suddenly dropped damage hurt shock tripped hit

1) _____.

2) _____.

3) _____.

2. *If you were telling someone else about the accident, would you use the same words and style no matter who you were talking to? Roleplay with your partner to practise two conversations with people who ask what happened: first with a friend and then with a police officer.*

3. *Now imagine that an ambulance arrives to take your friend to hospital. You have to explain what happened to the paramedic. Write down this conversation as a dialogue below. Try to include all of these words:*

x-ray   medication   unconscious   alcohol   overnight

A) _____.

B) _____.

A) _____.

B) _____.

A) _____.

B) _____.

4. *Think of occasions when you would need to give sympathy to someone. What things would you say? Practise 3 conversations with your partner.*

5. *Now imagine you are going to call your friend's mother to tell her what has happened, so she can come to the hospital. Practise with your partner first and then use the A-B format to write a dialogue.*

S14a | Intermediate Discussion Dialogues

Read the dialogue below and discuss whether you agree with A or B.

Taking a loan

A: I'm thinking of getting a bank loan. Have you ever thought of taking one out?

B: Yes! I took out a loan to pay for an anniversary holiday with my wife: what a great trip!

A: Have you paid it off yet?

B: No – but no rush! I don't earn very much but they gave me a good rate and the repayments are quite low.

A: Don't you think you should try and pay it off?

B: Actually I'm thinking of taking out another loan first, so we can have another big holiday!

A: Be careful! You'll end up stuck with debts you can't pay.

B: Don't worry – it'll be OK! Anyway, you've got to make the most of your life while you can…

Read the dialogue below and discuss whether you agree with A or B.

Youth crime rates

A: I had to get a taxi home last night because there were so many teenagers out by the bus stop.

B: I know what you mean – it's scary out at night sometimes.

A: Most of the time I'm sure I would be fine, but the trouble is that it only takes one of them to try something – and they all know they could probably get away with it!

B: Don't be so sure: the police do a good job – and there are lots of CCTV cameras on the streets now.

A: But even if they get caught, what's going to happen to them? We don't have strict enough penalties for theft and muggings!

B: Hmm. I'm not sure about that. Maybe we need to provide more things for them to do instead of hanging around on the streets at night. That way we could create a safer environment for us all.

Intermediate Discussion Dialogues

Look at the lines below from a dialogue between two people, A and B.
Try to put them in the order they would be used in their conversation.

A: But you might not find another job!
A: Oh, come on, get real! You can't force companies to do that!
A: How did your job interview go?
A: That's a shame. But surely that won't stop you taking the job?
A: That's great!

One of the things that is difficult about a real conversation is that it
is impossible to know what the other person is going to say to you!
However, it can help if you are able to predict what someone might
say response to your questions and comments...

Think with a partner about what B might say in the dialogue above.

B:
B:
B:
B:

Now can you put these lines from a different dialogue in order?

A: That's not the point! You must know that when you drink, your
   reflexes slow down.
A: Hmm. If you drive home from here I'm going to call the police
   as soon as you set off.
A: But you could have an accident and hurt someone else. What if
   you end up killing a child?
A: You'll certainly be over the limit!
A: Surely you're not driving home? After all those drinks?

Think with your partner about what B might say in this dialogue.

B:
B:
B:
B:

Intermediate Discussion Dialogues

Read the dialogue below and discuss whether you agree with A or B.

A nursery in the workplace

A: How did your job interview go?

B: Well, they offered me the job!

A: That's great!

B: Well, yes, but I haven't accepted it yet – there is one problem. I asked about their nursery for employees' children, but they said they are closing it this year.

A: That's a shame. But surely that won't stop you taking the job?

B: I could pay for a private nursery, but that would be so expensive that it's almost not worth going to work at all. And it would add to the time it would take me to get to and from work.

A: But you might not find another job!

B: Maybe – but I think all companies should provide a nursery for employees' children.

A: Oh, come on, get real! You can't force companies to do that!

Read the dialogue below and discuss whether you agree with A or B.

Reporting a friend for drink driving

A: Surely you're not driving home? After all those drinks?

B: Don't worry, I haven't had very many.

A: You'll certainly be over the limit!

B: It's all right, I won't get caught if I drive slowly.

A: That's not the point! You must know that when you drink, your reflexes slow down.

B: Well, I've never had any problems before.

A: But you could have an accident and hurt someone else. What if you end up killing a child?

B: I've told you, I'll be fine.

A: Hmm. If you drive home from here I'm going to call the police as soon as you set off.

S15 Intermediate Discussion Topics

Job Satisfaction

Look at the list below in pairs and discuss which factors have the greatest influence on job satisfaction and those which have the least. What other factors can you think of?

High Salary	Responsibility
Long Holidays	Chance to be creative
Chance to help people	Pleasant surroundings
Adventure	Prestige/Social status
Contact with people	Chance to travel
Job Security	Variety of day-to-day work

Who are you?

What makes you 'you'? Look at the list below in pairs and discuss the things which have had the greatest influence on making you who you are. What other things make the real 'you'?

Heredity	Experiences you have had
Your parents' example	Your education
Physical environment	The country you live in
Brothers and sisters	Media / TV / films and videos
Friends or colleagues	The music you listen to

In what ways do you think you might be different if some of these factors were different'?

Many of these factors are determined for us: what things can we influence in our own lives and what things are impossible to change?

S16 | Giving a Talk or a Presentation

All of the students are going to choose a topic of interest and give a talk to the class. You can choose a hobby, a famous person, a place, or anything else that you are interested in. Maybe you would like to talk about where you live or your own personal background.

Start making notes below to help you plan your talk.

Some ideas to help you:

Make notes to help you remember what you are going to say, but be careful not to simply read them aloud. You must be able to look at people's faces while you are talking.

Practise your talk with family or friends so that you do not hesitate too much, and so that you will not be too nervous when you stand at the front of the class and talk about your topic.

Plan different tenses and expressions which you can use in your talk. If you are able to, prepare something to show the class while you are talking.

Marking scheme: Your teacher will give you marks for these criteria.

Task
   (How well did you follow your instructions?)
Fluency
   (How well did you avoid hesitation and pauses?)
Accuracy
   (How accurate was your grammar and pronunciation?)
Eye Contact
   (How well did you look around the room at all the people listening?)

Linking Words, W1-W5

Linking words are the main building block of written sentences, and many issues with students' work can often be pre-empted by work in this area.

<u>W1</u> emphasises the use of 'and', 'but', 'because' and 'so' as linking words and as such it could be used with elementary levels or as a review activity for higher level students.

<u>W2</u> shows the importance of choosing the right linking word for the meaning you want to convey: contrast 'but' with 'so' in Question 1, for example. Students can then show their understanding of this in Questions 2 and 3 by writing sentences in context. Note that differentiating for lower level students may be necessary in Question 4 and that the use of 'because' and 'so' are interchangeable depending on the clause order.
The missing words are: but – but – because – but – so – but

<u>W3</u> reminds students that 'and' and 'but' are not usually used at the beginning of a sentence, and teaches the corresponding adverbial linking words for these conjunctions.

Note that it is not normally correct to use 'because' at the start of a written sentence: for example, 'I opened the window. Because I was hot.' However, you may want to go into some examples showing students the informal usage of 'because' at the beginning of a sentence, e.g. if it is not separated from its clause: 'because I was hot, I opened the window' (which is a pattern they should also recognise with 'when') and contrasting this with 'because of that' which is similar to 'therefore' and 'so'.

<u>W4</u> draws this point out further by highlighting that 'because of' and 'despite' are followed by a noun (which could be a gerund, a verb in the '-ing' form) whereas most linking words are followed by a full clause.

<u>W5</u> reviews the work covered in different contexts.

W1 | Linking Words

Join these sentences together using 'and' or 'but'.

I told her about your new job. She was very happy.

I started studying English two months ago. I like my teacher.

I work in the post office. I don't work on Saturday or Sunday.

We can also use 'because' or 'so' as linking words:

I didn't come to the party *because* I was feeling ill.

I was feeling ill *so* I didn't come to the party.

Choose the best linking word for the sentences below.

The table broke _____ the boy jumped on it.

James ran away _____ the man was chasing him.

The doctors tried to save her _____ she died last night.

My brother lost his book _____ he broke his mobile phone.

The man has been ill _____ we may hear bad news soon.

The driver stopped shouting _____ he was still very angry.

"I'm going to bed now _____ I'll switch off the lights."

I waited three months _____ my birthday present didn't arrive.

When you have finished, go back and try to add an adjective into each sentence. Some of the sentences are easier than others!

W2 Choosing your Linking Word

1 *How many linking words could you use to join these clauses together?*

> I need to study English _____ I work every day.

Notice that you can use different linking words in order to communicate a different meaning.

2 *Now choose a linking word for the sentence below and write a paragraph which includes your sentence.*

> I walked home _____ I was tired.

3 *When you have finished, use a different linking word and write another paragraph with the new sentence.*

4 *These sentences have been mixed up. Can you choose a linking word for each sentence and write it correctly?*

I brother like football sports love doesn't my.

is never my brother sister talking very stops shy my.

he hit road was didn't him that bicycle the check the clear.

the one have police caught might partner a think he thief they.

flowers say bought some needed he to wife he sorry his for to her.

boys hard all the of studied them test unfortunately not passed the.

5 *Now write a sentence of your own with a linking word. Then mix up the words and give it to your partner to make a correct sentence.*

W3 | Pre-intermediate Linking Words

One of your friends is studying English in the UK. The sentences below are all taken from a letter your friend has written to you. Can you match the first half of each sentence with the second half? Join the sentences together using these linking words: and, but, because, so.

1	The food is nicer than I was expecting	I can't speak English very well.
2	I have found a place to live	I was feeling really nervous.
3	It's difficult for me to make friends	I am still waiting to hear back from them.
4	Life is very expensive here	I am trying to find a job.
5	I went for one interview	the weather is quite warm.
6	I didn't enjoy the interview	I like the other people in my flats.

7 *Now can you match the meanings of the following words:*

and	therefore
but	what's more, in addition
because	however
so	the reason is (was) that...

Which column above contains words we usually use at the beginning of a sentence in written English?

8 *Now look again at sentences 2-6 in the letter from your friend. Which linking word could you use to start each of these sentences?*

9 *Finally, think of your own ideas and write some more sentences which you could add to the letter, using as many linking words as you can.*

W4 | Intermediate Linking Words

1. *Which words would you use in these gaps?*

He says he is such a careful driver that he refuses to use the radio in his car. _____, he had a crash last week when he drove home.

Now his insurance has gone up _____of the crash.

Or: Now his insurance has gone up _____ he had the crash.

Notice the grammatical difference between the last two sentences above.

2. *Now can you match the endings of these sentences correctly?*

He didn't go to the party despite   it was raining.
They went on their picnic even though   the weather.
He didn't go to the party even though   being invited.
They went on their picnic despite   he was invited.

3. *How many of the following sentences do not make sense?*

Despite losing my wallet, I had a great weekend.
Losing my wallet despite I had a great weekend.
I had a great weekend despite losing my wallet.
Even though I forgot my tickets, I got there on time.
I forgot my tickets even though I got there on time.

Can you correctly fill in the gaps below so these sentences have the same meaning as the correct sentences above?

I had a great weekend even though_____.

I got there on time despite_____.

4. *Some of the words below are very commonly used. Can you write a sentence for each one using it as a linking word?*

when   where   if   for this reason

on the other hand   furthermore

W5 | Advanced Linking Words

Choose a linking word from this box for each sentence below.

when	for this reason	if
on the other hand	furthermore	where

On the one hand that car is cheaper and much smaller; _____
_____ it might need a lot of repairs.

I just don't care _____ my boss finds out!

James stood up slowly _____ his name was called.

It's impossible to count the number of stars in the sky. _____
_____ we can say the universe is
beyond our full understanding.

They planted the tree in the place _____ the boy
had found his mother's diamond.

I promise to find the missing child. _____
I will make sure that we punish whoever was responsible.

*Now can you match these sentence halves together and then join them
with a suitable linking word?*

On the one hand I expect I'll put the phone down	the weather forecast.
	he calls again.
My mum moved to the area	
	they were really nervous beforehand.
The match went really well	
We will still go to the beach	she grew up as a child.

*Finally, can you add a second sentence to each idea, using a linking
word at the start of each of your sentences.*

Error Corrections and Punctuation, W6-W11

<u>W6</u> is actually a warm-up activity which can then be used to check students' grammar and sentence constructions. You can collect their finished sentences and then use them as an error correction activity or for a correct sentences auction game.

<u>W7</u> gives an example of a basic error corrections list. This is a very useful way to feed back authentic mistakes, in a way that ensures every member of the group has to focus on each item. For such a valuable teaching tool, it needs little preparation: set your group a short writing task, ideally just one paragraph, for example about a shop they often go to, or something they do at the weekends, then collect the work. Select sentence mistakes and write them on the board, or on pieces of paper to hand out in groups, or use individual word cards to focus on word order.

The set of sample sentences in W7 would be of use in review or as a launching pad into practising more difficult language, such as linking words. Note also that correcting the sentences when they are in a written format does not necessarily mean your students are able to use the same grammar in spoken work.

<u>W8</u> onwards is a focus on punctuation, with reference back to real texts which may be used before students try the task. Inverted commas (or speech marks) are a particular area that students often need to practise in their own written work.

<u>W9</u> includes some higher level punctuation, such as a dash, and a semi-colon, which your learners should try to use in their own work when carrying out the worksheet writing tasks.

<u>W10</u> specifically includes several instances of inverted commas as a part of a punctuation review. When discussing this story you can ask if students know traditional stories from their own culture, which may lead into a speaking or a writing activity.

<u>W11</u> also links back to authentic stories for self-checking of students work, although the reading texts are of an advanced level: if your students are not ready for the stories as a reading activity, you could nevertheless combine the punctuation review with teaching any new vocabulary from these texts.

W6	What Happened Next?

Fill in the end of each sentence and try to make a funny story.

Last Saturday, I went shopping in...

I was feeling happy because...

Suddenly, I saw...

One of the people in the shop looked...

There was only one thing I could do. Immediately I...

W7 | Proof Reading: Error Corrections

When you are writing English, you need to check your work when you have finished. It is easy to make mistakes with grammar, tenses, punctuation, and spellings, so you need to check all of these things.

Can you correct all of the mistakes in each sentence below?

Yesterday I went to shopping.

I got cloths for my children.

Then we went to saw my sister.

I eats lunch there every day thursday.

My brother always working, never there.

My brother becomes police officer when he was 25.

I gone shopping after lunch.

I went post office to paid my bills.

I bougt some food, I cookd dinner four my family.

Then I was clean my house.

Tomorrow I got appointment with doctor at 9 o'clock.

I no drink coffee last week because doctor say drinking too much.

I had to wake up early tomorrow.

But my favourite day of the week is saturday, so I can sleep late.

Now write about your favourite day of the week. Which day is it, and why? Be careful to check your work when you have finished.

W8 | Pre-intermediate Punctuation

Which sentence in a) to f) below should have:

1. an exclamation mark

2. a question mark

3. a full stop

4. another capital letter

5. an apostrophe

6. inverted commas

a. A student trip to Windsor Castle – what could go wrong

b. The classroom is much easier work every time

c. I brought that wallet, along with the students jacket, with me.

d. My students had all come to england from other countries.

e. Finally we could get started

f. Was yours on a green key ring?

Read the teacher's account of the student trip to Windsor Castle again. How many other forms of punctuation can you find? What do these different means of punctuation show?

Imagine you were one of the students on the trip to Windsor Castle. Write a letter to the teacher to say thank you for organising the trip: include all of the forms of punctuation in 1) to 6) above, and try to use other punctuation as well.

You will need to plan in advance all of the things you want to write, and the order of the paragraphs you will use in the letter.

| W9 | Intermediate Punctuation |

Match each form of punctuation with the best reason for using it.

an exclamation mark   to introduce an illustration of your point

a question mark   to show spoken words

a comma   to show a pause in the flow of a sentence

inverted commas   to ask a question

a colon   to mark urgent or surprising information

a semi-colon   to list or mark different parts of a sentence

a dash   to show an independent clause within a sentence

Re-write the following text using correct punctuation including capital letters, apostrophes, and full stops.

you cant wait for some bus rides to end every traveller can remember an arduous journey over a difficult mountain pass across a dusty plain or simply through endless countryside

but closing your eyes can hide away an unexpected moment of beauty who can know when a glimpse of the light may be enough to transform the earthly view into a heavenly one

stop the bus we couldnt simply drive past without taking pictures here the sudden view of the sparkling river set on the canvas of clear blue skies fresh with the mountain air was about to flash past our windows too quickly

Now write a short description of a beautiful place where you have been.

FYG photocopiable materials   No Limits – Unlimited

W10 | Punctuation

Read the following story and then re-write it with the correct
punctuation in the space below. Who do you think will win the race?

once there was a large rabbit whose name was harry he lived in a
forest one day he was very bored because all the other rabbits
had gone away while he was going for a walk he met one of his
friends whose name was tommy im bored said harry lets have a
race the first one to get to the park is the winner ok said tommy

harry was a hare and he ran very quickly but tommy was a
tortoise so he was very slow harry knew he was going to win
easily so he stopped for a rest he sat down under a tree where he
fell asleep

tommy was very slow but he didnt stop quietly he walked past the
tree where harry was sleeping

after a long time the hare finally woke up suddenly he
remembered the race oh no he thought i have to hurry he started
running to the park as fast as he could

When you have finished, think about the end of the story. Who do you
think wins the race? Write an ending for the story.

Punctuation Exercises

Look at each of these sections from the story 'English Breakfast', and copy out the sentences with correct layout and punctuation.

what about our food i complained and were never going to get to our b&b now don't worry well get there said tommy patiently itll just be later than we planned thats all its a chance to think of others who are needier than yourself

i squatted down in front of them can i help i asked gently taking her hands away from her face the lady said we have lost them our grandchildren her husband explained we let them go into the shop in the service station and now we haven't seen them since the explosion

eventually tommy came back how did you get on i asked excitedly that policewomans radio wasnt working properly for some reason he said shaking his head

Look at each of these sections from 'View From My Kitchen Window', and copy out the sentences with correct layout and punctuation.

ive seen some crises unfolding before my window my elderly neighbour was nearly mown down by a car screeching off the petrol forecourt somebody stole petrol silly really dont people know all petrol stations have signs saying all drive offs are reported to the police and cameras recording the licence plates

the window cleaner had come and gone i took my gloves off and sent a quick text to my husband i thought id finished the washing up but when i checked the kitchen id forgotten the pots and pans i had been cooking dinner with they were still on the stove food splattered and grimy

i didnt hear exactly what was being said but i discerned shouting and banging and witnessed the raider angrily gesturing to get his money this seemed to be happening in slow motion actually it took 35 seconds for him to storm in point a gun grab the cash and oddly a bottle of champagne storm out jump back into the focus insert the key and speed off

Punctuation Exercises

Look at each of these sections from 'Your E-mail or Your Wife?' Copy out the sentences with correct layout and punctuation.

jenn muttered quietly to herself and then continued with the tea she hardly saw stuart these days he didnt spend much time with the twins any more either when he said an office in the garden would be less distracting she never imagined how much time he would spend out there

jenn was really beginning to feel neglected if it wasnt for that stupid computer being in the house then she would probably never see him at all once the twins were in bed jenn went into the kitchen to make herself a drink she looked down the garden he was still in there she screwed up her face angrily and decided it was time she taught stuart a lesson

he walked over to the back door and pushed the handle down and then again it suddenly occurred to him that there were no lights on and then it dawned on him oh no what does she think shes playing at stuart moaned and cursed as he tried to think of an answer to his dilemma and then he noticed the small window in the bathroom was open

it was a long night and as stuart eventually calmed down he began to think about why jenn was so hurt and angry with him he started to realise that he hadnt paid her any attention for ages or ellie and alex he would make it up to them work would not be his top priority any more when jenn arrived home from work on thursday stuart was waiting for her with a cup of tea

jenn was speechless she wished that she had locked him out sooner friday was a beautiful day stuart climbed into the drivers seat of jenns car and they set off up the road in high spirits but it wasnt long before stuart glanced at the fuel gauge oh no jenn why didnt i remember how bad you are at filling your car up with petrol

Now write a paragraph explaining whether you agree or disagree with the following statement, giving your reasons:

Everyone should spend more time learning how to use a computer.

Look at each of these sections from 'Another Brian' and copy out the sentences with correct layout and punctuation.

as the sponge went moist in his mouth brian spotted a strange object buried within the depth of the cake before him it was a small burgundy box the type that would contain a ring or a set of cufflinks

as he entered the shop brian noticed a sweaty looking man in a dirty coat follow him into the store suspiciously pacing the aisles with his head bowed brian was about to pay for his petrol when the man grabbed his arm twisted it behind his back and forced him through the emergency exit

you mustnt give him that key why i dare not say well what if i say no the man took out a gun from his inside pocket and aimed at his own head then my life and eventually your life will not be worth living you threaten me with your life youre insane

brian panicked as he suddenly realised he was trapped he could hear the footsteps of his pursuer approaching he collapsed frustrated and breathless onto the park bench as the other man emerged from within the woods and raised the gun i need that key he shouted no why should i believe you

he thought for a long time before he realised what he must do ok he said decisively but first you'll have to take my handcuffs off the older man put his gun down with relief and bent over brians wrists to unlock him

Now complete this sentence below about yourself.

If I could travel in time, I would like to _____

_____

_____.

Finally write a paragraph explaining whether you agree or disagree with the following statement, giving your reasons:

Yesterday was for learning, today is for living, and tomorrow is for dreaming.

Punctuation Exercises

Look at each of these sections from 'The Emerald' and copy out the sentences with correct layout and punctuation.

the emerald restaurant towered dramatically against the inky sky the october landscape gave the impression of a delicate canvas a backdrop for the elaborate 1930s architecture of modern londons finest dining haunt

the other stars lay hidden in the wings delaying their arrival for fear of upstaging the undeniably gorgeous couple other mere mortals such as the two girls en route to their bus stop felt privileged even to cross this celebrity couples path one of the young women gasped an o of surprise while the other stared unashamedly

while eleanor was the picture of perfection in a pale pink chiffon dress with pink diamonds to match her date on the other hand seemed to prefer the understated look sporting tattered black jeans a shabby dinner jacket which upon closer inspection was merrily decorated with food stains and three days worth of stubble it was safe to say that the emerald restaurant had *never* in all its years seen a character such as jeremy francis descend its immaculate steps before

jeremy returned the compliment with a lopsided grin and melanie forgot to breathe sorry were late said eleanor dismissing these servers with her eyes but we couldnt shake everyone off after they were congratulating us on the show tonight we also made a quick stop at the petrol station on the way then of course once we got here we couldnt find a safe place to park jeremys motorbike mrs lipton gasped motorbike she whispered is something wrong mother eleanor asked

Now write a paragraph about yourself, starting with this sentence. Choose 'would' or 'would not'.

I would / would not like to be a celebrity because_____

_____.

Finally write a paragraph explaining whether you agree or disagree with the following statement, giving your reasons:

It is easier to enjoy life if you are neither too rich nor too poor.

Describing Pictures, W12-W14

<u>W12</u> depends on you being able to find a picture to use in class which includes at least one of these sentences, so as to incorporate the true or false activity. The activity is easily adapted, however, to suit a different picture that you may be able to use: in such a case, of course, you may want to focus on a different grammar point instead of the present continuous.

<u>W13</u> is a cut-up worksheet, with the top half being seen by only one student in each group. The reading is used by that student as a dictation, but it has both spelling and grammar mistakes in it: you will need to choose which student will be the reader in the group depending on your circumstances, and during the first reading, students attempt to draw the scene being described. They then write out the sentences when it is read to them again. (You may want to choose a different reader for this stage.)

If the reader finds a grammatical mistake as they are dictating, they can try to correct it as they read, but listeners also need to try to correct any mistakes they notice. After finishing the text, all the students in the group should compare their versions, and discuss the spellings together. After this stage you can hand out the corrected text, for the group to check together thoroughly. Note that one aim of this activity is to emphasise the importance of accurate pronunciation, for example: 'quite' or 'quiet'.

<u>W14</u> is a follow-up where students now have to draw their own picture of a scene which will be suitable for a picture dictation... this is a fun activity if students grasp the concept since they need to draw their own picture first, and then write a suitable description of it in the space on their worksheet.

You can then choose appropriate texts to pass to other groups, for one student to read, and for his or her partners to attempt to draw. Note that students should now be familiar with the need to simultaneously check for mistakes as they read or write the dictation, as introduced in W13. What's more, you can try to mark these texts by the time of the next lesson, in order to lead a feedback activity, and you may also be able to photocopy the original pictures drawn by the students who wrote those descriptions, so students can compare their own versions.

W12 Writing About a Picture

Put each set of words in order to make a correct sentence. Then write in the box on the right whether that sentence is true or false for the picture your teacher gives you.

shopping a in the is supermarket woman   *True or False?*

a are at the many waiting for train people station

children playing beach the are on there some

mobile on man is his talking phone one

new young bicycle a there a boy is riding

beautiful are people the and weather swimming some is

When you have finished, write some more sentences about your picture.

Picture Dictations

Read this text slowly so that the other members of your group can draw what you describe. You will find some mistakes in the text: if you notice grammatical mistakes, try to correct them while you are reading, but you can discuss spelling mistakes together when you have finished.

There are two childrn and two adults in the picture who is siting under a tree eating lunch. The mum and dad have taken their two boys for a picnic in a park.

They are all happy because it sunny. The boys are having funn so he smiling. One of is eating appl and his brother drinkking milk.

One boy wering a new t-shirt and the other boy has got a jumper on. They has both got short hair.

Their mother is waring a flowery dress and she going to take a photo with an camera. Her hair is quiet long.

Their father is wearing shorts and sunglases but he isn't eat food.

When you read the text again, the members of your group have to write down these sentences. Then you can discuss all of the mistakes together.

Did you find all of the mistakes? Check your work here.

There are two *children* and two adults in the picture who *are sitting* under a tree eating lunch. The mum and dad have taken their two boys for a picnic in a park.
They are all happy because it *is* sunny. The boys are having *fun* so *they are* smiling. One of *them* is eating *an apple* and his brother *is drinking* milk.
One boy *is wearing* a new t-shirt and the other boy has got a jumper on. They *have* both got short hair.
Their mother is *wearing* a flowery dress and she *is* going to take a photo with *a* camera. Her hair is *quite* long.
Their father is wearing shorts and *sunglasses* but he isn't *eating any* food.

W14 | A Picture Dictation of Your Own

Now you are going to make your own picture dictation. Other members of your class will have to try and draw a picture from your description later.

First you need to draw your picture here. Use ideas which can easily be drawn in a picture:
for example, car, bus, table, chair, house, window.

Now write sentences below to describe your picture. Remember that someone else will have to draw what they hear in this description, so you need to explain your picture very clearly – and in the best order.

Constructing Sentences, W15-W17

W15-W16 Link to S12, W17 to R9-R13

Dictation activities are a very useful teaching technique, and it is always one of the most interesting of activities for eliciting from students why they are doing it... It is of course a listening activity, including elements of deductive understanding, but it is also a writing activity which requires students to understand how sentences are constructed – especially if you do not give in to their pleas to read a sentence 'just once more'!

A basic dictation can be long or short and read out by the teacher. Even if not specifically designed as a review of grammar or vocabulary covered in class, it will nonetheless work as a valuable consolidation of students' knowledge.

W15 is a means of carrying out a dictation as a gapfill activity to differentiate for students of varying level or ability, but there are other creative ways of carrying out dictations.

W16 gives the full text for students to check their answers to the gapfill exercise but it could also be used for a paired dictation: give the text to one student in each pair, to read it for their partner, and when they have finished, the students swap roles. You can differentiate further by choosing which gapfill version each student fills in, although I would normally give the more difficult worksheet to the second student in a pair, i.e. the one who has already read the text. Again this technique can work very well with a short dictation.

W17 is another means of helping students with constructing sentences. These sentences relate back to the authentic short story texts in R9 to R13, but the gapfills have been chosen in order to review common areas such as articles and possessives which may trouble students in their own written work.

Word order is often a difficulty for students, who may form sentences completely differently in their own language. One way to reinforce English word order is therefore to use mixed up sentences such as those in the W17 worksheet. As always the same technique can be used to meet your students' specific needs, but remember that unless you set written work to mark, you have never truly checked their progress.

Gapfill Dictation: Julie's Birthday

Listen to the dictation and fill in the gaps. Remember to include punctuation.

I _____ Wales _____ child.

My _____ there _____ country

when _____ but _____ York. I____ lived

here _____ in a small flat _____ soon

after _____ here. I _____ miss

the _____ Welsh hills _____ lot

of _____ countryside here, _____ everything

I _____ including _____ people.

Yesterday _____ birthday _____ a

big _____ great – even _____ they

all _____ made _____ my

age. _____ had

in _____ my _____ some

school _____ party and it was

the _____ life _____ glad

to be _____ wondering _____.

Gapfill Dictation: Julie's Birthday

Listen to the dictation and fill in the gaps. Remember to include punctuation.

I _____ child. My

parents _____ when

I_____York.

I _____ flat

that _____ here.

I _____is

a _____ here,

and _____ the

chance _____.

Yesterday _____ big

party _____they

all _____ jokes

about _____ I

ever _____ birthday

some _____ it

was _____ to

be _____.

W16   A Birthday Party

Read the following text by Julie about memories of her best birthday.

I used to live in Wales when I was a child. My parents moved there to a house in the country when I was five but now I live in York. I've lived here for twelve years in a small flat that I bought soon after I arrived and I'm really happy here. I don't miss the beautiful Welsh hills because there is a lot of lovely countryside here, and the city has everything I need including the chance to meet new people.

Yesterday it was my thirtieth birthday so I had a big party with all my friends. It was great – even though they all brought birthday cards which made jokes about my age. It reminded me of the first party I ever had in our house in Wales. On my tenth birthday some school friends came for a party and it was the happiest day of my life because I was glad to be so old. Now I'm wondering how I can stay young.

What happens at a birthday party? Write about a birthday of yours: it could be your most recent one or a memory from your childhood.

W17a   Constructing Sentences

Look at each of these sentences from 'English Breakfast' and choose a suitable word for each of the gaps.

1. Hungry, we decided to stop at _____ next motorway service station.

2. We were evacuated into _____ field away from _____ service station building.

3. As she sat on _____ bench she put _____ head in _____ hands.

4. We let _____ go into the shop in _____ service station and now we haven't seen _____.

5. I sat on _____ bench with them and talked to _____ old lady.

6. I caught _____ glimpse of _____ blue baseball cap emerging from _____ police car.

7. The gentleman handed Tommy _____ key. "Take it. Borrow _____ key as our way of saying thank you."

Now can you re-order these words to make sentences from the story?

1. arrived scene the vehicles emergency on.

2. out elderly I the noticed of an come couple woods.

3. to my up I them immediately place offer jumped.

4. tried companion to looked her worried as he pale and console her.

5. an it for was like he age away seemed.

6. excited towards two were running tall boys there and us.

W17b Constructing Sentences

Look at each of these sentences from 'View From My Kitchen Window' and choose a suitable word for each of the gaps.

1. It's not a view onto _____ back garden and we don't have _____ front garden. It's a view which keeps _____ in touch with _____ world as I wash up. _____ view is the hustle and bustle of _____ street outside _____ front door.

2. My other neighbour is _____ elderly blind man. I hear_____ gentle tapping of _____ stick mapping out _____ door and step for him. I knock on _____ kitchen window; he turns, smiles and waves.

3. There is_____ gap between two of _____ homes, and through this narrow passageway is_____ local park. I often take _____ stroll that way and eat_____ Twix on _____ park bench, watching_____ children swing higher and higher.

4. I took note _____ every car that graced _____ station that afternoon; _____ sapphire blue Focus caught_____ eye.

5. I took _____deep breath and held onto the edge of _____ sink to steady myself and collect_____ thoughts, which seemed to swim before _____ eyes.

Now can you re-order these words to make sentences from the story?

1. other she we each smile passes as at.

2. all I and do sees the station it so petrol.

3. was garage our frozen sink when I pull still to a car the into heard I.

4. I've what never seen you'll just guess.

5. in Focus I've the locked garage the.

W17c | Constructing Sentences

Look at each of these sentences from 'Your E-mail or Your Wife?'
Choose a suitable word for each of the gaps.

1. Stuart looked down at _____ shiny new key in _____ hand.
It was _____ key to _____ own space; somewhere _____
could have peace and quiet to do _____ work. He turned
_____ key in _____ keyhole and then admired _____ brand
new office, in the form of _____ shed.

2. Jenn waited _____ he had returned to _____ office and
then she locked _____ back door, turned off _____ lights
and went _____ bed.

3. Stuart wasn't going _____ take _____ chances, _____ he
pulled into _____ nearest petrol station, but he _____ determined
that nothing _____ going _____ spoil _____ day.

4. "Roxford Park! We _____ been _____ for ages. I wonder if our
bench _____ still standing," exclaimed Jenn, and _____ rushed
out of _____ car.

5. "I'm so glad it's _____ here," she said, running _____ fingers
over _____ etched heart that contained _____ names.

Now can you re-order these words to make sentences from the story?

1. email in check popped my I've to just.

2. Stuart she these saw days hardly.

3. time he more with spend didn't twins any much the either.

4. it realised was after late it well midnight when how Stuart was.

5. the open window he small bathroom was in noticed the.

6. round to and put arm her sat his Stuart her next.

W17d Constructing Sentences

Look at each of these sentences from 'Another Brian' and choose a suitable word for each of the gaps.

1. Brian cut _____ a large triangle and shovelled _____ sloppily _____ his mouth _____ a child _____ devour _____ .

2. Brian was about _____ pay _____ his petrol when _____ man grabbed his arm, twisted _____ behind _____ back and forced him through the emergency exit.

3. Before Brian _____ speak he _____ hurled through the open rear doors _____ a transit van parked at _____ back _____ the petrol station.

4. There was _____ slight resemblance which _____ Brian briefly wonder _____ this assailant _____ related.

Now choose a suitable word for each of the gaps in these sentences from 'The Emerald'.

1. The star dimmed _____ a moment as _____ winking.

2. Melanie arrived with _____ genius plan that granted _____ an acceptable reason to _____ the table _____ visit: she presented the four _____ them _____ complimentary drinks _____ the house, praising Jeremy for _____ she had _____ heard from other diners to _____ been a fine stage debut.

Can you re-order these words to make sentences from 'The Emerald'?

1. up their managed first already tables to had mixing Simon's it day two orders offend was and he by

2. find a park course Jeremy's we then couldn't got of safe to once here we motorbike place

3. number he was to count discovered required it firmly tape inspection into strips to able of fix after close the he of that place

Informal and Formal Letters, W18-W22

W22 Link to S5

W18 contains a letter that your students imagine they have received, and can be used as both a review of writing an informal letter and an error correction exercise. Note that these corrected sentences can also be used as a model to help students with subject-plus-verb sentence construction.

W19 could be cut in half to set students two different tasks at different times. This worksheet works very well, however, if you are able to mark their first letter and then set the second letter as a follow-up assignment. It is important to expect learners to implement the feedback that you give them, so make clear that you will be looking specifically at the areas for improvement you have highlighted in the first piece of work.

W20 needs to be folded (or cut in half!) so that students first try to fill in the 'page' in the top section of the worksheet, with the second half available to them later for reference.

W21 mainly emphasises the issue of appropriate language and expressions used in a formal letter, but also provides a framework for paragraphing. A useful task for students is therefore to identify the main purpose of each paragraph, and then use this as a plan for drafting their own re-written version of the letter.

W22 contains two other kinds of formal letter, which could be set as an initial task and a follow-up, in the same way as W18, or they could be treated entirely separately.

Note that complaint letters are a specific type of letter in which it is very important to document all the background detail, and it is necessary for the writer to make clear what redress or compensation they are expecting as a result of the complaint.

Meanwhile, as students progress to longer pieces of work, they should be encouraged to plan their writing: at lower levels, learners need to focus on the construction of individual sentences, but as this skill develops, they can concentrate on improving the overall flow of their work, for example by deliberately ordering and linking their paragraphs.

W18 Penfriend Letters

Read this letter from a new penfriend.

> Hi, how are you? My name is Sandeep.
>
> I live in London in my older uncle house. I have two bedroom in a flat. I study in college, there I have a lot of friends. I have not job. It's quite and many shopping in my area.
>
> It's wonderful the life in London. I've here for four years my impressions are really good. The buses runs 24 hours every day and very easy. The food also very good and many restaurants. London it's very nice city to visit. England has so many sports playing here like golf, cricket, rugby.
>
> Please write to me and tell me about where you live.
>
> Your friend,
>
> Sandeep

Discuss these questions in pairs.

How old do you think Sandeep is?

How good is her English?

Do you think she is sometimes sad in London?

Would you enjoy living abroad or would you prefer to stay at home?

Can you correct the mistakes in these sentences from Sandeep's letter?

1. I live in London in my older uncle house.
2. I have two bedroom in a flat.
3. I study in college, there I have a lot of friends.
4. I have not job.
5. It's quite and many shopping in my area.
6. It's wonderful the life in London.
7. I've here for four years my impressions are really good.
8. The buses runs 24 hours every day and very easy.
9. The food also very good and many restaurants.
10. London it's very nice city to visit.
11. England has so many sports playing here like golf, cricket, rugby.

W19 | Informal Letters

Pen pal letter

You are going to write a short letter introducing yourself to a pen pal in the UK. Ask your new friend some questions, and include as much information about yourself as you can, including these ideas.

- When and where you were born.
- How old you are.
- Your family.
- Where you live.
- Why you want to learn English.

Thank you letter

Last week your friends invited you to a party to celebrate your birthday. You are going to write a letter to one of your friends to thank them for their present, and for organising the party. Tell him or her what you enjoyed the most and why.

| W20 | Formal Letter Layout |

Where do you need to put the following in the layout of your letter? Write them in the correct place on the 'page' opposite.

My address

My name

The recipient's address

Dear…

Yours…

Introduction

My signature

Final greeting / request

Main body of letter

Date

My name	My signature	Yours…	Final greeting / request	Main body of letter	Introduction	Dear…	Date	Recipient's address	My address

Look at the letter below. Then try to re-write it so that the content and language is more appropriate for a formal letter to the UK embassy. Remember to use the correct layout and sign the letter.

Hi Mr Visa Person,

I found out on the internet that I can write to you to get a visa for the UK.

I want to go to the UK some time next year and I want an application form! My parents have got enough money to pay for me and I won't cause any trouble when I am there.

There are lots of things I want to study and I think every university in the UK would want to have me as a student – especially Oxford and Cambridge.

I've passed all the English exams I've ever taken, although it is difficult to understand people talking fast in English. But anyway I am the best student in the class (you can ask anyone!) and I know I'll pass all of my English exams at the end of this year.

I want to come to the UK because it will be a good way to get a good job when I am older and I hope I will meet lots of people. All my friends will be so jealous!

Call me any time and we'll sort out a good date for me to have an interview if I need to have one. I know I will be a good student. Just take a look at my references.

Thanks and hope to see you soon!

W22 | Formal Letters

Letter of complaint

You recently went on a plane journey and you are very dissatisfied with the service. The flight was delayed although no announcement was made to explain why. On the plane you were not served with any drinks, and when you arrived you found out your bags were missing. Now you are going to write a letter of complaint to the airline.

Remember to include:
- *Your reason for writing*
- *Background information and details of the problems*
- *What result you expect*

Proposal letter

You have heard about a local government project to improve local facilities in the area where you live. They have asked residents to write to them with suggestions which will benefit the community. You are going to write a letter making a proposal.

You could include the following ideas:
- *Why you are writing and where you heard about this project*
- *Details about your suggestion*
- *The ways this would improve the local area*

Job Letters, W23-W25

A job application letter is also a specific form of letter which needs to refer back to the advertisement you have seen. Note that in real life it is important to check the requirements specified in a job advert, such as necessary experience or qualifications, so as not to waste time with a futile application.

W23 has been produced with two versions so that you can choose the relevant one for your situation, either in the UK or abroad: ask students whether this would be a good job to apply for, and if so, why – most students should meet the personality specification and no experience is necessary.

The advert asks for a CV, known as a résumé in the USA, and for this students should be able to present their personal details, education, qualifications and skills, employment history, interests, and give a reference.

W24 suggests one approach for helping students to learn set phrases. Although memorisation of set phrases is of limited use in spoken English, as it does not simulate a conversation, this method may help some students with written work, especially if they are from a learning culture which uses rote learning.

Students try to memorise the content of these short letters and then attempt to re-write them word for word, but the overall objective is that they use the exercise to choose which phrases or chunks of the letter are worth learning in this way. Note also that the sample letter is an application for a different job, meaning that you can set students the task of applying for the job in W23 as a follow-up consolidation activity: they should be able to write a more detailed covering letter referring back to the criteria in the advert. Meanwhile it would be a constructive exercise for students to roleplay an interview for this job giving examples of their trustworthiness and ability to take initiative.

W25 is set in the context of having got the job in W23, and assesses students' ability to leave a note for someone: the main idea with this task is for students to be able to convey the main information in a succinct but polite way.

W23 | Shop Assistant Application Letter

Look at the job advertisement below. Read the criteria that the shop is looking for and then draft a covering letter for your job application.

CUSTOMER LIAISON ASSISTANT - local area.
GOOD SALARY.

We are a new English-speaking shop seeking a hard-working local individual for liaison with customers. No experience necessary. You must be able to speak and read English well, preferably with the ability to use a computer. You will carry out duties as assigned by the Shop Manager, including communicating with suppliers; you must be trustworthy and able to look after the shop on your own when necessary. The ability to work under your own initiative is essential. Possibilities for advancement and trips abroad in the future. Apply with your CV and a covering letter to:

The Personnel Manager, Hollywood Comes to Town
Address:

IMPORTS AND SHOP ASSISTANT - airport area.
SALARY £15-20,000 pa.

We are a fair trade company seeking a hard-working individual for a role in an expanding shop. No experience necessary. You must be able to speak at least one foreign language from an Asian, African, Middle Eastern, or European country, preferably with the ability to use a computer. You will carry out duties as assigned by the Shop Manager, including communicating with suppliers, and clearing imports at airport customs. You must be trustworthy and able to look after the shop on your own when necessary. The ability to work under your own initiative is essential. Possibilities for advancement and trips abroad in the future. Apply with your CV and a covering letter to:

The Personnel Manager, Imports Come to Town
Address:

W24 | Application Expressions and Phrases

1 *Look at the text of this letter and underline the most useful phrases.*

Dear Sir or Madam,

I am writing to enquire about the position of Administration Officer which I saw advertised in last week's Employment Weekly News.

I would be very grateful if you could send me an application form.

Yours faithfully,

Melanie Williams

2 *Now turn over the page and try to write the same letter from memory.*

3 *It is useful to be able to use formal phrases in an important letter or email. There are, of course, different ways of saying the same thing, however. Which of the following phrases could be used in a letter?*

… which I saw advertised in…   … which I saw advert in…
… which advertised in…   … which was advertised in…
… which got advertised in…   … which I noticed in…

4 *Now read this letter and underline the most useful phrases.*

Dear Mr Jenkins,

I am writing to apply for the position of Administration Officer. Please find my application form enclosed.

As you will see from my application I have IT qualifications and I can speak two other languages in addition to English. I am a hard worker and I am willing to learn new skills.

I trust my application will be of interest and I look forward to hearing from you.

Yours sincerely,

Melanie Williams

5 *Turn over the page and try to write the same letter from memory.*

6 *What differences did you notice between the two letters?*

7 *Now write a letter using some of these formal phrases in a new situation.*

W25 | Writing a Short Note

You are now working in a shop with other English speaking people.

You are looking after the shop on your own while the manager is on lunch break but you get an emergency phone call and you have to leave the shop urgently. There are no customers in the shop so you will lock the door because the manager also has a set of keys.

You have to write a note to the manager below, explaining that you are going out for a short time – make sure you say why, and when you will be coming back.

Advanced Writing Skills, W26-W28

W26 uses a text which students may read in a personalised context, and is an assessment of summarising skills. A written summary of a text is a good challenge for students as it not only requires comprehension, but also the ability to reproduce the main information in the writer's own words. An exercise like this can be particularly valuable as it requires a learner to construct written sentences to express something they may find easier to communicate verbally.

The gapfill task should be done after folding the worksheet, as it replicates the full text. The teacher has an important role here in preventing the task from simply being a memory exercise: one way to do this is to encourage alternative answers, as long as adjectives, nouns, and verbs are used in the correct places.

W27 provides a framework for students to plan a story: since the elements of a plot will lead to the interaction of different tenses, in both narration and dialogue, a written story is a comprehensive language task, and will also enable you to thoroughly assess the strengths and weaknesses of your students' written work.

The worksheet steers students through a process of building up their story with a partner and is designed to let the writer develop the background to their story as well as the plot: in essence, the plot of a student's story needs to introduce a 'problem' for the characters, and then explain what happens as a result...

W28 is a step-by-step introduction to writing a biography of a famous person. An assignment like this can incorporate many skills, including research techniques, and writing a draft. The work is pointless, however, if you are unable to persuade students not to copy information from books or the internet: be clear that you will only mark work written in students' own words.

For this reason you might choose instead to emphasise the speaking tasks in the worksheet, and set students the task of presenting their findings in a spoken format. If so this would also enable you to introduce your students to the principles of note-taking, in which case you could collect the notes students take during the presentations made by other members of their group.

W26 | Summarising the Main Information from a Text

1 *Read the following text from an article about self-study techniques.*

Some people find it difficult to work when there is background noise. It can be very distracting when there are cars or workmen outside your window, or if there is a radio playing in a nearby flat or garden.

On the other hand, some people like listening to music when they are working. It may be easier to listen to instrumental music than the lyrics of songs, but there are many people who insist that listening to a CD of their favourite pop band actually helps them concentrate.

It is also important to be comfortable and alert when you are working. It is difficult to work well if you are too hot or too cold, and the quality of your work will suffer if you try to work when you are too tired because it is easy to make small mistakes without noticing.

2 *Now turn your paper over and write a summary of this article. You do not have to use the same words, but you need to try to include all the main points in the text.*

- -

3 *Look at the text below and try to fill in the gaps with an appropriate word.*

Some people find it _____ to work when _____ is _____ noise. It can be very _____ when there are cars or workmen _____ your window, or if there is a radio _____ in a _____ flat or garden.

On the other _____, some people like listening to music when they are working. It _____ be _____ to listen to instrumental music than the _____ of songs, but there are _____ people who _____ that listening to a CD of _____ favourite pop band actually helps them _____.

It is also _____ to be comfortable and _____ when you are _____. It is difficult to work well if you are too hot or too cold, and the _____ of your work will _____ if you try to work when you are too tired because it is _____ to make small mistakes without _____.

W27 Writing a Story

Think of a book or a film you have enjoyed. Explain the main events of that story to a partner.

Write short answers for these questions about the story you enjoyed.

How did it start?
Who was it about?
What problems did they have?
What was exciting about the story?

Now match these sections of a basic story with the descriptions given.

Beginning		we find out about a problem the characters face
Middle		we find out whether they solve their problem
End		background about the characters in the story

Next, you are going to make a plan for a short story of your own. Write some notes using the following questions to help you.

Who is the main character in your story?
What information do we know about them?
Who are the other people in the story?
Where does the story happen?
How does the story start?
What main problem do the characters have?
What is exciting about your story?

When you are ready, show your notes to your teacher. Then work with a partner, and think about any improvements you might be able to make in each other's story.

Next, write your plan in full with a beginning, a middle, and an end.

When you have finished your plan, you are ready to write your story.

W28 | Writing a Biography

We are all interested in famous people: sometimes because they are entertainers and sometimes because we are inspired by what they have achieved.

What basic information do you ask someone when you meet them for the first time? Write down some of the questions you would ask.

Write down the names of two or three famous people. How much basic information (including your ideas above) do you know about them?

Choose one of the famous people your partner has listed. How much do you know about them? Think of questions you would ask them if you were going to interview them on a radio programme.

Now roleplay your interview with your partner. You will do two interviews: one of them when you are the celebrity, and one of them when you are the interviewer.

Next you are going to draft a plan for a biography you will write about a famous person. Use the ideas above to help you decide what information you are going to include. Since this is a draft, you can leave gaps where there is information you might need to find out later. Then you can use a book or the internet to research these points before completing your final article. However, it is very important that you use your own English.

Do not copy sentences from any other source.

Examples and Ideas for Assessment, T1-T7

The worksheets in this section are intended to be self-explanatory for students, as reviews of work that has already been covered.

Assessment is an essential part of teaching, and the process of monitoring and checking must never be overlooked: a teacher is continually analysing which students have understood what, and how much more time is needed on any part of the lesson plan. In addition to this ongoing daily process, students need formative assessment: the semi-formalised combination of tests and marked work which enables both the teacher and the student to see how far the student has progressed, and what areas still need work. This is in contrast to summative assessment, which is a formalised process to determine what a student has achieved, usually at the end of a course, resulting in a specific qualification.

These worksheets should therefore be used formatively, with the results being fed back to students to let them know how well they are progressing, and what they need to do to improve. The worksheets include ideas for testing vocabulary and word order as well as grammar, and as always the ideas behind these materials can be adapted into simple worksheets of your own.

T1 covers instructions and basic future tenses.

T2 reviews some specific vocabulary as well as basic past tenses and verbs followed by another verb with either 'to' or '-ing'.

T3 reviews 'would like' and comparatives and superlatives.

T4 covers various phrasal verbs including vocabulary.

T5 is a page of active-passive and passive-active transformations.

T6 includes a further review of passives as well as conditionals.

T7 is a gapfill review of tenses, which could be photocopied in two sections and / or supplemented with a list of verbs to choose from.

T2 | Vocabulary and Tenses

Can you fill in these missing words?

1. If you speak a language very well, you speak it f_____ .
2. Bread which is old is s_____ .
3. A person who is caring and helpful is k_____ .
4. Someone who is not rude to people is p_____ .

Now make sentences using the following words.

1. whale _____ .

2. orphanage _____ .

3. running water _____ .

4. luxury _____ .

Can you change the verb in brackets to the correct tense?

A) Sorry I'm late! Have you _____ (wait) long?

B) Not too long. I haven't _____ (read) all of the newspaper yet.

A) And the bus was late. There _____ (be) an accident near the pub, which they are still clearing up.

B) What _____ you _____ (do)? You look tired.

A) Cleaning the house. I _____ just _____ (finish).

Now complete these sentences using verbs with either 'to' or 'ing'

1. The man threatened _____ .

2. My mum urged me _____ .

3. Let's carry on _____ .

4. The shopkeeper promised_____ .

Pre-intermediate Grammar Review

Can you match together the sentence halves below and then write the full sentences correctly?

Stephen football like a	like in a o'clock five please
would coffee please	my a friends window like please
likes my chocolate	would for birthday his
and I near table would the	wife much very
I'd taxi at morning the	some like I

Look at the mixed up sentences below. One word is missing from each sentence – you must choose a word from the box so that you can complete the sentences correctly.

1. faster a car a is than.
2. than salad is a chips fresh.
3. much Africa is than hotter.
4. more city a is beach a than.
5. than bus walking a cheaper is.
6. grandmother is my than my older.
7. are roads than country motorways.
8. relaxing is driving than a more train a.
9. the one in is of sweetest world honey the.
10. one the Scotland world of countries in the beautiful is.
11. watching computer exciting than sport is playing games.

car	Europe	bicycle	catching	most	more
	foods	healthier	peaceful	slower	cousin

T4 | Phrasal Verbs

Put the words in the right order to complete these sentences.

1. The inspector got on the train while I _____ .
   (my/ was/ for/ looking/ ticket)

2. Oh no! We've _____ . (milk/ run/ of/ out)

3. If you're hot you can _____ off. (tie/take/your)

4. At Heathrow, about 1000 planes _____ .
   (take/ day/ every/ off)

5. Could you just _____ for a
   minute? (after/ my/ baby/ look)

Select five correct phrasal verbs from the box and write a sentence for each of the ones you choose. Which ones are not real phrasal verbs?

> make up/ run over/ set up/ get over/ hang off/ take over/ join off/ take up/ get up/ set on /make in/ run away/ join in/ hang on

1. _____ .

2. _____ .

3. _____ .

4. _____ .

5. _____ .

6. *You may know many other phrasal verbs which use different combinations of the same words above. Try and write a one-paragraph story about two people, using as many phrasal verbs as possible.*

| T5 | Review of Passive Forms. |

Re-write the sentences below so that the second sentence has the same meaning as the first.

1. The whole city felt the earthquake
   The earthquake _____ by the whole city.

2. I think Russia will build the first house on the moon.
   I think the first house on the moon _____

   _____.

3. Your book was taken by my brother.
   My brother_____.

4. The policeman stole my car keys.
   My car keys_____ .

5. The accident was seen by the bus driver.
   The bus driver _____ .

6. We were told to wait at the station.
   Someone_____.

7. A profit of £250,000 has been reported this year.
   The company_____.

8. We will develop technology further in the future.
   Technology _____ .

9. People kill elephants in the mountains every year.
   Elephants _____.

10. They were serving drinks when we arrived.
    Drinks _____.

11. People in that village have always spoken Swahili.
    Swahili _____.

T6   Intermediate Tenses

Change these sentences to give the same meaning using passive forms.

1. The policeman stole my car keys.

2. Someone has broken the window.

3. Our teacher is cooking lunch today.

4. People kill leopards and tigers for their beautiful furs.

5. They will close the road because of the bad weather.

What if?

1. If I go to America, I _____ (get) a job.

2. What _____ you _____ (do) if your flight home was cancelled?

3. Water freezes if the temperature _____ (go) below zero.

4. If he read the newspaper, he _____ (know) what is happening.

5. I _____ (go) to Australia if my brother lived there.

6. If they help us, we _____ (be able to build) a new community hospital.

7. I _____ (study) very hard if I get a university place in the UK.

8. If I liked jazz music, I _____ (have) a party at the jazz club.

9. *What would you do if you won £100,000? Write five sentences about how you would spend the money. How much would you spend on each idea?*

T7 | Review of Tenses

Look at this dialogue: can you complete the conversation using suitable verbs in the correct tense? Where do you think the four friends are, and what day of the week do you think it is?

Anna) What are you _____ this evening, Ben?

Ben) I don't know. Maybe I _____ watch TV.

A) Do you _____ you_____ give me a lift to the station?

B) Er, no problem. _____ you _____ Eric tonight?

A) Yeah, he'_____ in London all of this week on business.

B) OK, it _____ good to see him.

Carol) Anna _____ really _____him,_____ you?

A) It's the first time we'_____ a week apart since we _____ married.

C) I bet you'_____ about him the whole time!

A) Yeah! And he only _____ me once this week.

C) What?! I hope he'_____ a good excuse!

A) He _____ take his clients out in the evenings – or so he says!

B) I'm sure he _____ you a few text messages every day.

A) Yeah, he _____. But they're not the same as _____ his voice.

Dave) Hi – sorry I'm late! _____ anyone _____ any more coffee?

- -

What tenses haven't they used in this conversation so far? Continue filling in the dialogue, starting when Dave comes back with a cup of coffee...

C) So what _____ to you, darling? _____ everything all right?

D) Yeah, fine. I _____ just _____ work when my boss _____ me.

C) Oh no, _____ you _____ another international client?

D) No, don't worry! So, Anna, how's Eric? ____ he _____ back today?

A) Yeah, he'_____ his newspaper on the train at the moment!

D) Do you need me to _____ you to the station later?

A) Thanks, Dave, but it's OK. Ben _____ take me.

D) Great. Well, maybe we'_____ you both tomorrow.

Index

Index of Reminders: the following items could have been mentioned on every page, and so they are listed here as a final reminder!

Dan Lamb has also written a novel:

THE MYTHS OF TURRET ROCK

Dan Lamb had his sights set on writing a novel ever since leaving university. This book took him five years to write, between teaching day and evening classes as a college ESOL lecturer.

"Amazing powers of imagination and storytelling."

"Emotive, sometimes shocking; delightfully full of suspense."

"A real page-turner, a wonderful adventure in a world with similarities to Orwell's 1984."

"A dramatic ending and a fantastic book."

"Exciting, challenging, thought-provoking."

How could such a creature as a whale have truly existed?

Very few people in this society of slaves and informers have ever seen the awe-inspiring waves...
   ... until a new punishment is instituted at Turret Rock.

Hermanus loves the sea and is plunged into the unexpected constraints and realisations of the life he has always wanted; will he then risk being persuaded that the whales really did exist – or are they just an imaginative story from the past?

Truth or myths? A multi-faceted dilemma of loyalties.

Searching for his brother,
   the culture shock of a new life;
      how old do you have to be for freedom?

Published by Fygleaves: New authors revealing their leaves to the world